CONTENTS

Sundays, in my childhood home, my father took over the cooking, giving my mother a much needed break. He would often serve a post-Church brunch of pancakes or waffles — and they were always an experiment of some kind or another. I look back at that time and thank my father for giving me the gift of experimenting with food and searching for new and different ideas.

This book is dedicated to my parents, Jean and Dick Rathmell.

INTRODUCTION

While most people think about using a waffle iron on a leisurely day (such as Sunday) for fresh waffles with syrup and maybe even fresh berries, the fact is that waffles can actually be quite a diverse food for any day of the week. For instance, try any of your favorite creamed chicken or beef dishes over a whole grain waffle for an absolute treat and change-of-pace supper. Top a corn waffle with chili for a delicious meal-in-minutes. Any dish which would normally be served over rice or noodles may be served with waffles — imagine beef Stroganoff over a whole wheat waffle or a Welsh rarebit served with a ham or meat waffle! We enjoy whole grain waffles with turkey soup. You can even use waffles in place of bread when making your favorite sandwiches!

Additions to waffles are unlimited -- try waffles with fruits, vegetables, nuts, chocolate, spices, cheeses, and even meats. The recipes in this book will serve as a springboard for your imagination in waffle making.

Your first reaction may be to avoid waffles made with yeast as the leavening agent instead of the more common baking powder. Proofing the yeast is not as difficult as you may think and it is, in fact, a quicker way to get waffles to the table in the morning, as most of the batter is prepared the evening before. Give it a try!

Waffle toppings themselves may be varied. Don't limit yourself to maple syrup — try waffles with applesauce, fresh fruit, yogurt, whipped cream or any of the delicious toppings provided for you in this book.

If you love waffles but don't have the time to prepare them in the morning before you're on your way to work or school, try making them on the weekend. They can be cooled and then heated before serving. Or freeze them and then heat them in your toaster or oven (350° for 5 minutes or so). In this way you can enjoy homemade waffles, hassle-free, on the run.

Waffle irons, like sandwich makers, may also be used to cook eggs. My children love their "waffled eggs" and consider them to be a real treat. Use your waffle iron to make an interesting French toast -- great for brunch entertaining, as it "dresses up" the meal. You can even use your waffle iron to heat up a regular sandwich, giving it an interesting waffled texture. I would suggest creamy-type fillings for this as opposed to meat fillings.

QUESTIONS AND ANSWERS ABOUT WAFFLE MAKING

What is the difference between a pancake batter and a waffle batter?

A waffle batter is usually a little thinner than a similar pancake batter. It will have more melted butter or vegetable oil than a pancake batter so that the resulting waffles will not stick to the iron itself. In addition, a waffle batter may have more eggs and/or sugar than pancake batter.

Can I use a favorite pancake batter in my waffle iron?

With some adaptations, a pancake batter may be used as a waffle batter. I would recommend either doubling the amount of fat (melted butter/margarine or vegetable oil) or using 3-4 tbs. of the fat. (4 tbs. equals ¼ cup). In addition to the fat adjustment, you should beat the egg white until stiff and fold in at the very end of your batter preparation for a fluffier waffle. If there is no egg called for in your pancake recipe, use one egg per cup (or close to) of flour. While this is a general rule of thumb, it may take some experimenting with your recipe so be sure to keep notes for the next time.

Can I use these waffle recipes for pancakes?

Yes, again with some minor modifications. I would recommend cutting the fat (melted butter, margarine or vegetable oil) in half. For thinner pancakes use a little extra liquid and for thicker pancakes use a little extra flour. The egg may or may not be separated and the white beaten and folded in at the end — that is your preference. The beaten egg white adds fluffiness to the results. Ladle the batter onto a hot griddle or frying pan and cook until bubbles appear. Turn the pancake over and cook until done (a golden color).

How much batter should I use for each waffle?

Pour or ladle approximately ⅓-½ cup (follow the guidelines provided by the manufacturer of your machine) of the batter into the middle of your hot, seasoned waffle iron. Cook waffles for 2-5 minutes or until golden brown and done.

What is the difference between a Belgian waffle and other waffles?

A Belgian waffle has deeper, thicker pockets which is the result, purely, of the type of waffle iron used. A Scandinavian waffle is usually heart-shaped, again, from the type of waffle iron. All recipes in this book will work in any of these different types of waffle irons.

The waffles sometimes stick. What should I do? It's so hard to clean the iron.

Follow manufacturer's guidelines for treating or seasoning the iron. If no information is available, season it by brushing melted butter, margarine or vegetable oil onto the cooking area in order to prevent sticking.

How do I know when the waffle is completely baked?

The waffle iron will stop steaming and will be opened easily. If there is any resistance to opening the iron, wait another half-minute or so and then try again.

Should the ingredients be at room temperature or warm when I make the batter?

With the exception of the egg and melted butter, all other ingredients may be taken directly from the refrigerator. You may, in fact, actually have better results if the ingredients are cool as the cooler temperatures restrict the development of gluten in the flour. In other words, there is a lesser probability of overbeating the batter if the ingredients are cooler.

Some recipes result in thin batters and others are thicker. Is this normal?

Yes. A thin batter will generally result in a tender waffle. A thick, rich batter will result in a crisp outside and a tender inside. Both are delicious.

Is it possible to freeze leftover waffles?

Absolutely! Any homemade waffle may be frozen and reheated just as you would a purchased frozen waffle. Simply allow the waffle to cool on a wire rack (I use the racks in the cold oven as an easy, out of the way place). When the waffle is completely cool, wrap in plastic or a plastic bag and freeze. Simply remove the frozen waffles and heat in your toaster, toaster oven or your conventional oven (350° for about 5 minutes). It is just as easy as the purchased variety but infinitely better and contains the ingredients you have decided you want or need.

Can these recipes be made more dietetic?

To adapt any recipes in this book to "diet recipes," you may try the following:

1. Increase the liquid (milk, juice, fruit puree) by approximately 2 tbs. This is to replace liquid lost by decreasing melted butter (or vegetable oil). If decreasing a sugar substitute such as honey or molasses, you may want

to increase the liquid a little more.

2. Decrease the fat (butter, margarine or vegetable oil) to approximately 1 tbs. Due to the lessened fat, make sure your waffle iron is well seasoned; otherwise the waffles may have a tendency to stick to the iron.

3. Decrease sugar, honey or molasses to ½-1½ tsp. (or to taste). If decreasing honey or molasses, you may need to increase the liquid (see above) by another tablespoon or so.

4. Sugar substitutes such as NutraSweet, etc., generally may not be used in recipes which are baked. If using a substitute such as fructose, use approximately ⅓ the amount of sugar (which includes honey or molasses) given. For example, if you are cutting the sugar to 1 tsp., use ⅓ tsp. of fructose. Fructose is available at your local health food store.

I enjoy fresh, hot, homemade waffles but really do not like separating and beating the egg. Is it really necessary?

The stiffly beaten egg white folded into the batter helps make the waffles tender and fluffy. Waffles without the beaten egg are less tender and fluffy but may still be delicious. If you decide not to beat the egg and are happy with the results, by all means do so.

What should I do if the batter looks too thin?

If the batter looks too thin and runny, add a few tablespoons to ¼ cup of flour. Too thin a batter will result in a limp waffle. However, keep in mind that a waffle batter is a relatively thin, pourable batter. You don't, however, want it too thin so that it just runs between the iron's grids.

What should I do if the waffles seem limp?

This could be due to not cooking long enough or too much liquid in the batter. Different flours and grains absorb moisture at varying levels. While the recipes usually give one specific amount, some minor adjustments may be required. Add flour one or two tablespoons at a time. You should never need to add more than ¼ cup (4 tbs.) of flour as the ratio of flour to water could be jeopardized. Up to ¼ cup, however, is generally safe. I find that oats, in particular, often require additional flour to be added.

What should I do if the waffles are tough and hard?

This is probably the result of overbeating the batter. The batter should only be mixed until the ingredients are just blended. It will be a lumpy batter but the lumps will bake out. It might help to use milk or juice which is cold instead of at room temperature.

It could also be that the waffles are being overcooked. Waffles are usually cooked when the steam stops and/or when the waffle iron is easily opened.

Can I use your recipes with self-rising flour?
Absolutely. If at least ¾ of a cup of all purpose flour is called for, substitute the self-rising flour, and omit the salt and baking powder from the recipe.

I need to make waffles for a crowd. How can I do that with these recipes?
All of the recipes in this book can easily be doubled.

What should I do if the waffles are pulling apart or taking a long time to cook?
Most probably the waffle iron has not been preheated properly and/or the iron is being opened too soon. Make sure that the iron is preheated properly and do not open it during the first minute or two of baking - definitely not before the steaming stops.

What are some other serving suggestions for waffles?
Most people equate waffles with breakfast or brunch using a syrup. There are several different ways to vary the serving of waffles:

1. Serve basic or whole grain/cereal waffles as a base for any food which would be served with rice or noodles.
2. Serve waffles with ice cream, whipped cream or Creme Fraiche for dessert. Fresh fruit could be served also.
3. Use waffles as the bread for sandwiches. I would recommend using a basic or whole grain waffle for this.
4. Vary the toppings used - see *Toppings,* page 142, for ideas.
5. Waffles could also be used as a base for pizza. Top with pizza sauce, grated mozerralla and other toppings if desired; place in broiler until cheese melts.

What are some other uses for my waffle iron?

Many people use their waffle irons to make French toast. It's an easy, hot breakfast food. The resulting French toast has the expected waffle pattern for holding favorite syrups or other toppings. Some batter ideas for French toast (approximately 2 slices) include:

Regular French Toast
1 egg, beaten
2-3 tbs. milk or cream
dash cinnamon or nutmeg

Orange French Toast
  1 egg, beaten
  1-1½ tbs. orange juice
  1-1½ tbs. milk
  ⅛ tsp. orange peel

Eggnog French Toast
  ¼-⅓ cup eggnog
  dash cinnamon or nutmeg, optional

Combine the given ingredients and place in a bowl which is approximately the same shape and size as your bread. Let the bread sit in the mixture for a minute or so on each side so that it soaks up the mixture (as opposed to just dipping it in). Place the bread in the preheated waffle iron and heat for 2-3 minutes or until golden brown.

In addition to French toast, some people make delicious, interesting sandwiches in their waffle irons. Use a sandwich filling which is creamy as opposed to those with meats, cheeses or vegetables. For example, use fillings similar in texture to peanut butter and jelly, cream cheese and chutney, deviled ham/tuna and mayonnaise. Place your filled sandwich in the waffle maker and heat for approximately 2-3 minutes. The resulting sandwich will have the waffle imprints making it an interesting sandwich to serve and eat! (Of course if you enjoy hot sandwiches of unlimited varieties, you may use a sandwich maker which is so designed. See my book, *The Sandwich Maker Cookbook* for approximately 200 hot sandwich ideas).

Cook bacon in your waffle iron along with your waffles, French toast or regular toast. Simply place on top of the waffle batter (French toast or even plain bread) a single piece of bacon which has been cut into two or three equal pieces. Heat in the waffle iron for approximately 3 minutes. Serve with your favorite syrup or topping. Note that the bacon drippings cook into the waffle, so make sure you allow it to cook long enough. Otherwise the results will be greasy.

Some people even cook scrambled eggs in their waffle irons. Make sure that the iron itself is well seasoned. Cook scrambled eggs with cheese or well diced, cooked meats such as bacon, turkey, ham or even ground beef. The eggs should cook until well set, approximately 2-3 minutes.

WHITE FLOUR, CHEESE AND MEAT WAFFLES

BASIC WAFFLE

This basic recipe makes a wonderful, light and fluffy waffle.

1 egg, room temperature and separated
1 cup all purpose flour
1 tsp. baking powder
1/8 tsp. salt
1 tbs. sugar
3/4 cup milk
4 tbs. butter or margarine, melted and cooled

Beat egg white in a small bowl until stiff and set aside. Mix together dry ingredients and set aside. Combine egg yolk, milk and melted butter. Add to dry ingredients, mixing until just blended. Fold in beaten egg white until just mixed. Do not overbeat batter.

BASIC WAFFLE — CAKE FLOUR

3-4 waffles

The cake flour adds extra fluffiness to this basic waffle.

1 egg, room temperature and separated
1¼ cups cake flour
1 tsp. baking powder
⅛ tsp. salt
1 tbs. sugar
⅔ cup milk
4 tbs. butter or margarine, melted and cooled

Beat egg white in a small bowl until stiff and set aside. Mix together dry ingredients and set aside. Combine egg yolk, milk and melted butter. Add to dry ingredients, mixing until just blended. Fold in beaten egg white until just mixed. Do not overbeat batter.

"DIET" WAFFLES

Even those of us who are constantly battling the bulge deserve waffles as a treat. Here is a relatively low-calorie recipe.

1 egg, room temperature and
   separated, or ¼ cup egg substitute
1 cup all purpose flour
1 tsp. baking powder
½ tsp. sugar

⅛ tsp. salt
9 oz. skim milk (9 oz. equals ¾ cup
   plus 2 tbs.)
1 tbs. melted margarine or butter

If using an egg, beat egg white in a small bowl until stiff and set aside. Mix together dry ingredients and set aside. Combine egg yolk, milk and melted butter. Add to dry ingredients, mixing until just blended. Fold in beaten egg white until just mixed. Do not overbeat batter.

If using egg substitute, mix together dry ingredients and set aside. Combine egg substitute, milk and melted butter. Add to dry ingredients, mixing until just blended. As the amount of butter is significantly decreased from the normal amount, make sure that the waffle iron is well seasoned. You may use a nonstick spray unless specified by the manufacturer's directions.

Note: If you wish to try to adapt any recipe in this book to be more dietetic, please see suggestions on page 6.

SWEET BUTTER WAFFLES

Wow! Delicious, sweet, rich waffles for a decadent start to the day. Not meant for those days when you're counting calories.

1 egg, room temperature and separated
1 cup all purpose flour
1 tsp. baking powder
⅛ tsp. salt
2 tbs. sugar
⅔ cup milk, room temperature
6 tbs. butter or margarine, melted and cooled

Beat egg white in a small bowl until stiff and set aside. Mix together dry ingredients and set aside. Combine egg yolk, milk and melted butter. Add to dry ingredients, mixing until just blended. Fold in beaten egg white until just mixed. Do not overbeat batter.

HONEY WAFFLES

3-4 waffles

A sweet variation on a basic waffle. For a real treat, serve with plain honey, honey spread or any of the honey toppings provided in **Toppings,** *page 142.*

1 egg, room temperature and separated
1 cup all purpose flour
1 tsp. baking powder
⅛ tsp. salt
⅔ cup milk
2 tbs. honey
4 tbs. butter or margarine, melted and cooled

Beat egg white in a small bowl until stiff and set aside. Mix together dry ingredients and set aside. Combine egg yolk, milk, honey and melted butter. Add to dry ingredients, mixing until just blended. Fold in beaten egg white until just mixed. Do not overbeat batter.

BUTTERMILK WAFFLES

A relatively low-calorie waffle. The thick batter rises well and makes a quite delicious waffle.

1 egg, room temperature and separated
1 cup all purpose flour
1 tsp. baking powder
⅛ tsp. baking soda
⅛ tsp. salt
1 tsp. sugar
1 cup buttermilk
2 tbs. butter, melted and cooled

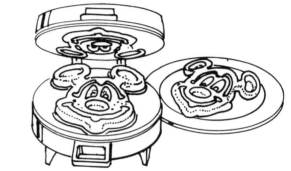

Beat egg white in a small bowl until stiff and set aside. Mix together dry ingredients and set aside. Combine egg yolk, buttermilk and melted butter. Add to dry ingredients, mixing until just blended. Fold in beaten egg white until just mixed. Do not overbeat batter.

EGGNOG WAFFLES

A tasty holiday season treat. A relatively thick batter.

1 egg, room temperature and separated
1 cup all purpose flour
1 tsp. baking powder
1/8 tsp. salt
1/8 tsp. cinnamon
1/16 tsp. nutmeg
1 tbs. brown sugar
3/4 cup eggnog
4 tbs. butter or margarine melted and cooled

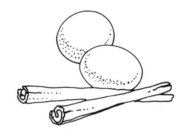

Beat egg white in a small bowl until stiff and set aside. Mix together dry ingredients and set aside. Combine egg yolk, eggnog and butter. Add to dry ingredients, mixing until just blended. Fold in beaten egg white until just mixed. Do not overbeat batter.

SWEET CREAM WAFFLES

A wonderful, rich waffle. Serve with any of the delectable toppings found on pages 142-152.

2 eggs, room temperature and separated
1 cup all purpose flour
1 tsp. baking powder
2 tbs. sugar
1/8 tsp. salt
3/4 cup heavy cream (whipping cream)
4 tbs. butter or margarine, melted and cooled

Beat egg white in a small bowl until stiff and set aside. Mix together dry ingredients and set aside. Combine egg yolks, cream and butter. Add to dry ingredients, mixing until just blended. Fold in beaten egg whites until just mixed. Do not overbeat batter.

LEMON CREAM WAFFLES

Wow! This is a "must try." Milk may be used in place of the cream, if desired.

1 egg, room temperature and separated
1 cup all purpose flour
1 tsp. baking powder
⅛ tsp. salt
1 tbs. sugar
1 tsp. lemon peel
⅔ cup cream
2 tbs. lemon juice
4 tbs. butter or margarine, melted and cooled

Beat egg white in a small bowl until stiff and set aside. Mix together dry ingredients and set aside. Combine egg yolk, cream, lemon juice and butter. Add to dry ingredients, mixing until just blended. Fold in beaten egg white until just mixed. Do not overbeat batter.

MAPLE WAFFLES

Enjoy the maple syrup baked right into the waffles!

1 egg, room temperature and separated
1¼ cups all purpose flour
1 tsp. baking powder
⅛ tsp. salt
¾ cup milk
2 tbs. maple syrup
3 tbs. butter or margarine, melted and cooled

Beat egg white in a small bowl until stiff and set aside. Mix together dry ingredients and set aside. Combine egg yolk, milk, syrup and melted butter. Add to dry ingredients, mixing until just blended. Fold in beaten egg white until just mixed. Do not overbeat batter.

MALTED MILK WAFFLES

A slight taste of malt gives this waffle a unique flavoring. Malted milk powder is usually found with dry milk products in your grocery store.

1 egg, room temperature and separated
1 cup all purpose flour
1 tsp. baking powder
⅛ tsp. salt
1 tbs. sugar
3 tbs. malted milk powder
¾ cup milk
4 tbs. butter, melted and cooled

Beat egg white in a small bowl until stiff and set aside. Mix together dry ingredients and set aside. Combine egg yolk, milk and melted butter. Add to dry ingredients, mixing until just blended. Fold in beaten egg white until just mixed. Do not overbeat batter.

COCONUT CHOCOLATE CHIP WAFFLES

3 waffles

A well loved combination. Serve with chocolate or maple syrup. These waffles may be enjoyed for either a rich breakfast or dessert.

1 egg, room temperature and separated
1 cup all purpose flour
1 tsp. baking powder
⅛ tsp. salt
⅓ cup coconut flakes
¾ cup coconut cream (canned)
4 tbs. butter or margarine, melted and cooled
⅓ cup chocolate chips

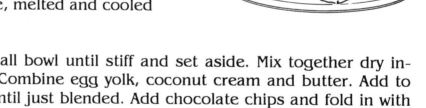

Beat egg white in a small bowl until stiff and set aside. Mix together dry ingredients and set aside. Combine egg yolk, coconut cream and butter. Add to dry ingredients, mixing until just blended. Add chocolate chips and fold in with beaten egg white until just mixed. Do not overbeat batter.

WHITE CHOCOLATE WAFFLES

Here's another waffle you won't be able to resist. The vanilla and white chocolate combination is superb.

1 egg, room temperature and separated
1 cup all purpose flour
1 tsp. baking powder
⅛ tsp. salt
1 tbs. sugar
⅔ cup milk
2 tsp. vanilla extract
4 tbs. butter or margarine, melted and cooled
⅓ cup white chocolate or vanilla chips

Beat egg white in a small bowl until stiff and set aside. Mix together dry ingredients and set aside. Combine egg yolk, milk, vanilla and butter. Add to dry ingredients, mixing until just blended. Add white chocolate chips or vanilla chips and fold in with egg white until just mixed. Do not overbeat batter.

M&M WAFFLES

This is for all the "M&M-aholics" of the world! May be served with ice cream or simply enjoyed "as is."

1 egg, room temperature and separated
1 cup all purpose flour
1 tsp. baking powder
⅛ tsp. salt
2 tbs. brown sugar
¾ cup milk
1 tsp. vanilla extract
4 tbs. butter or margarine, melted and cooled
⅓ cup M&Ms (I use plain)

Beat egg white in a small bowl until stiff and set aside. Mix together dry ingredients and set aside. Combine egg yolk, milk, vanilla and butter. Add to dry ingredients, mixing until just blended. Add M&Ms and fold in with beaten egg white until just mixed. Do not overbeat batter.

BUTTERSCOTCH WAFFLES

3 waffles

These are absolutely sumptuous. The combination of coconut and butterscotch makes these one of the best.

2 eggs, room temperature and separated
1 cup all purpose flour
1 tsp. baking powder
⅛ tsp. salt
1 tbs. brown sugar
¼ cup coconut flakes
¾ cup evaporated milk
4 tbs. butter or margarine, melted and cooled
⅓-½ cup butterscotch chips

Beat egg white in a small bowl until stiff and set aside. Mix together dry ingredients and set aside. Combine egg yolks, milk and butter. Add to dry ingredients, mixing until just blended. Add butterscotch chips and fold in with beaten egg whites until just mixed. Do not overbeat batter.

ALMOND BRICKLE WAFFLES

3 waffles

I use the packaged "Bits 'O Brickle" for these wonderful dessert waffles. Heath Bars could also be crushed and used. Serve with ice cream.

1 egg, room temperature and separated
1 cup all purpose flour
1 tsp. baking powder
⅛ tsp. salt
2 tbs. brown sugar
⅔ cup milk
2 tsp. vanilla extract
4 tbs. butter or margarine, melted and cooled
⅓-½ cup almond brickle chips or Heath Bar pieces

Beat egg white in a small bowl until stiff and set aside. Mix together dry ingredients and set aside. Combine egg yolk, milk, vanilla and butter. Add to dry ingredients, mixing until just blended. Add candy chips and fold in with beaten egg white until just mixed. Do not overbeat batter.

CHEDDAR CHEESE WAFFLES

2-3 waffles

A wonderful cheesy flavor. The cheese thickens the batter of this high-rising waffle. Great cooked longer for added crispiness.

1 egg, room temperature and separated
1 cup all purpose flour
1 tsp. baking powder
1/8 tsp. salt
1 tbs. sugar
3/4 cup milk
4 tbs. butter, melted and cooled
1/2 cup cheddar cheese, grated

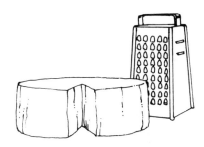

Beat egg white in a small bowl until stiff and set aside. Mix together dry ingredients and set aside. Combine egg yolk, milk, melted butter and cheese. Add to dry ingredients, mixing until just blended. Fold in beaten egg white until just mixed. Do not overbeat batter.

COTTAGE CHEESE WAFFLES

Rises nicely to a fluffy waffle. Rich in taste. Best if cooked longer than normal so it's a little crispier.

1 egg, room temperature and
   separated
1 cup all purpose flour
1 tsp. baking powder
⅛ tsp. salt
1 tbs. sugar

⅛ tsp. baking soda
¾ cup milk
½ cup cottage cheese
4 tbs. butter or margarine, melted
   and cooled

Beat egg white in a small bowl until stiff and set aside. Mix together dry ingredients and set aside. Combine egg yolk, milk, cottage cheese and melted butter. Add to dry ingredients, mixing until just blended. Fold in beaten egg white until just mixed. Do not overbeat batter.

Variation: YOGURT OR RICOTTA WAFFLES
Use yogurt or ricotta cheese in place of the cottage cheese.

SOUR CREAM WAFFLES

4 waffles

An incredibly light and tender waffle. Not meant for counting calories!

4 eggs, separated
1 cup all-purpose flour
1 tsp. baking powder
1/8 tsp. salt
1/3 cup sugar
8 oz. sour cream (equal to 1 cup)
4 tbs. butter or margarine, melted and cooled

Beat egg whites in a small bowl until stiff and set aside. Mix together dry ingredients and set aside. Combine egg yolks, sour cream and melted butter. Add to dry ingredients, mixing until just blended. Fold in beaten egg whites until just mixed. Do not overbeat batter.

POTATO WAFFLES

A fluffy waffle with a delicate taste of potato.

1 egg, separated
1 cup all purpose flour
1 tsp. baking powder
1/8 tsp. salt
1 tbs. sugar
1/2 cup mashed potatoes
3/4 cup potato or regular water
4 tbs. butter or margarine, melted and cooled

Beat egg white in a small bowl until stiff and set aside. Mix together dry ingredients and set aside. Combine egg yolk, potatoes, water and melted butter. Add to dry ingredients, mixing until just blended. Fold in beaten egg white until just mixed. Do not overbeat batter.

BLUE CHEESE WAFFLES

Serve "as is" with a green salad for a complete meal. If desired, use whole wheat flour instead of the all purpose.

1 egg, room temperature and separated
1 cup all purpose flour
1 tsp. baking powder
1/8 tsp. salt
dash garlic powder
1/2 tsp. sugar
3/4 cup milk
1/2 cup blue cheese, crumbled
1-1 1/2 tbs. finely diced red onion
2 tbs. butter or margarine, melted and cooled

Beat egg white in a small bowl until stiff and set aside. Mix together dry ingredients and set aside. Combine egg yolk, milk, cheese, onion and butter. Add to dry ingredients, mixing until just blended. Fold in beaten egg white until just mixed. Do not overbeat batter.

BACON WAFFLES

This is a true winner. For added bacon flavor, cut a slice of bacon (uncooked) into two or three pieces and place on top of the batter prior to heating. Heat a minute or two longer than normal, allowing the bacon to cook. You'll be coming back for more of these.

1 egg, room temperature and
  separated
1¼ cups all purpose flour
1 tsp. baking powder
⅛ tsp. salt

1 tbs. brown sugar
¾ cup milk
4 tbs. butter or margarine, melted
  and cooled
½ cup cooked, crumbled bacon

Beat egg white in a small bowl until stiff and set aside. Mix together dry ingredients and set aside. Combine egg yolk, milk and butter. Add to dry ingredients, mixing until just blended. Add bacon and fold in with beaten egg white until just mixed. Do not overbeat batter.

Variation: CHEDDAR CHEESE AND BACON WAFFLES
Add ½ cup grated cheddar cheese when you add the bacon.

BROCCOLI AND CHEESE WAFFLES

3 waffles

A superb, light waffle to serve at a brunch. Top with melted cheese and garnish with broccoli. I encourage you to use the caraway.

1 egg, room temperature and separated
1 cup all purpose flour
1 tsp. baking powder
⅛ tsp. salt
1 tsp. sugar
½ tsp. caraway seed, optional
¾ cup milk
½ cup grated Swiss cheese
¼ cup cooked broccoli florets
4 tbs. butter or margarine, melted and cooled

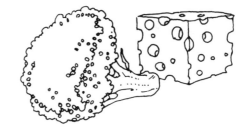

Beat egg white in a small bowl until stiff and set aside. Mix together dry ingredients and set aside, adding caraway seed if desired. Combine egg yolk, milk, cheese, broccoli and butter. Add to dry ingredients, mixing until just blended. Fold in beaten egg white until just mixed. Do not overbeat batter.

MEAT WAFFLES

Use leftovers for these waffles, which make a great lunch or supper, served with soup and/or salad. Or, serve with a slice of tomato and Welsh Rarebit.

1 egg, room temperature and separated
1¼ cups all purpose or whole wheat flour
1 tsp. baking powder
⅛ tsp. salt
1 tsp. sugar
1¼ cups all purpose or whole wheat flour
¾ cup milk
2 tbs. butter or margarine, melted and cooled
½ cup cooked, diced ham, turkey or chicken

Beat egg white in a small bowl until stiff and set aside. Mix together dry ingredients and set aside. Combine egg yolk, milk and butter. Add to dry ingredients, mixing until just blended. Add meat and fold in with beaten egg white until just mixed. Do not overbeat batter.

WESTERN WAFFLES

An outstanding brunch or light lunch waffle. May be served with a salsa if desired.

1 egg, room temperature and separated
1 cup all purpose flour
1 tsp. baking powder
1/8 tsp. salt
1/2 tsp. sugar
3/4 cup milk
1/4 cup grated cheddar cheese
1-1/2 tbs. finely diced red onion
3 tbs. finely diced green pepper
1/4 cup cooked, crumbled bacon
4 tbs. butter or margarine, melted and cooled

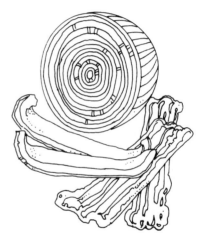

Beat egg white in a small bowl until stiff and set aside. Mix together dry ingredients and set aside. Combine egg yolk, milk, cheese, onion, pepper, bacon and butter. Add to dry ingredients, mixing until just blended. Fold in beaten egg white until just mixed. Do not overbeat batter.

MEXICAN WAFFLES

For a real change-of-pace dinner, serve these waffles with melted cheese and jalapeños.

1 egg, room temperature and
  separated
½ cup all purpose flour
½ cup cornmeal
1 tsp. baking powder
⅛ tsp. salt
1 tsp. sugar

⅔ cup milk
¼ salsa
½ cup ground meat cooked with
  taco seasoning*
4 tbs. butter or margarine, melted
  and cooled

Beat egg white in a small bowl until stiff and set aside. Mix together dry ingredients and set aside. Combine egg yolk, milk, salsa, meat and butter. Add to dry ingredients, mixing until just blended. Fold in beaten egg white until just mixed. Do not overbeat batter.

*The envelope of taco seasoning is normally used with 1 lb. of ground meat. For convenience, I cook the whole amount and freeze portions for later use.

GREEK CHEESE AND SPINACH WAFFLES   3 waffles

Serve these unique waffles for lunch or a light dinner with a Greek salad.

1 egg, room temperature and separated
1 cup all purpose flour
1 tsp. baking powder
1/8 tsp. salt
1/2 tsp. sugar
dash garlic powder
1/4 tsp. dill, optional
3/4 cup milk
1/3 cup crumbled feta cheese
1/3 cup cooked, drained, chopped spinach
4 tbs. olive oil, or butter or margarine, melted

Beat egg white in a small bowl until stiff and set aside. Mix together dry ingredients and set aside. Combine egg yolk, milk, cheese, spinach and oil. Add to dry ingredients, mixing until just blended. Fold in beaten egg white until just mixed. Do not overbeat batter.

ITALIAN SAUSAGE WAFFLES

3 waffles

This is a very light, crispy waffle. Try this: Top with pizza sauce and grated mozzerella cheese, place under the broiler until cheese melts and enjoy a special pizza!

1 egg, room temperature and
  separated
1¼ cups all purpose or whole wheat
  flour
⅛ tsp. salt
½ tsp. sugar

1 tsp. basil or oregano, or 1 tbs.
  fresh
1 tsp. baking powder
¾ cup milk
2 tbs. butter or margarine, melted
  and cooled
½ cup cooked, diced Italian sausage

Beat egg white in a small bowl until stiff and set aside. Mix together dry ingredients and set aside. Combine egg yolk, milk and butter. Add to dry ingredients, mixing until just blended. Add sausage and fold in with beaten egg white until just mixed. Do not overbeat batter.

Variation: COUNTRY SAUSAGE WAFFLES
  Replace the Italian sausage with country or breakfast sausage, and omit the basil or oregano.

WHOLE GRAIN, CEREAL AND SPICE WAFFLES

WHOLE WHEAT WAFFLES

3-4 waffles

In addition to breakfast, this is a great waffle for lunch or supper. Serve with soup and/or salad.

1 egg, room temperature and separated
¾ cup whole wheat flour
¼ cup wheat bran
2 tbs. wheat germ
1 tsp. baking powder
⅛ tsp. salt
¾ cup milk
1 tbs. honey
2 tbs. butter, melted and cooled

Beat egg white in a small bowl until stiff and set aside. Mix together dry ingredients and set aside. Combine egg yolk, milk, honey and melted butter. Add to dry ingredients, mixing until just blended. Fold in beaten egg white until just mixed. Do not overbeat batter.

HEALTHY WHOLE GRAIN WAFFLES

3 waffles

Use these waffles as a base for a delightful sandwich or meal.

1 egg, room temperature and separated
½ cup whole wheat flour
⅓ cup oats
¼ cup oat bran
2 tbs. wheat germ
1 tsp. baking powder
⅛ tsp. salt
¾ cup milk or water
1 tbs. honey
2 tbs. butter or margarine, melted and cooled

Beat egg white in a small bowl until stiff and set aside. Mix together dry ingredients and set aside. Combine egg yolk, milk or water, honey and butter. Add to dry ingredients, mixing until just blended. Fold in beaten egg white until just mixed. Do not overbeat batter.

SEVEN OR NINE GRAIN WAFFLES

3-4 waffles

This recipe makes a medium to thick batter which rises nicely, and produces a crunchy, flavorful whole grain waffle.

1 egg, room temperature and separated
1 cup whole wheat flour or all purpose flour
½ cup 7 or 9 grain cereal
1 tsp. baking powder
⅛ tsp. salt
¾ cup milk
2 tbs. honey
4 tbs. butter or margarine, melted and cooled

Beat egg white in a small bowl until stiff and set aside. Mix together dry ingredients and set aside. Combine egg yolk, milk, honey and melted butter. Add to dry ingredients, mixing until just blended. Fold in beaten egg white until just mixed. Do not overbeat batter.

Note: 7 or 9 grain cereal is available in health food stores, by mail order, or some larger grocery stores.

CEREAL WAFFLES

The cereal adds both flavor and crunch - a real delight.

1 egg, room temperature and separated
3/4 cup all purpose flour
1 cup cereal flakes
1 tsp. baking powder
1/8 tsp. salt
1 tsp. sugar (white or brown)
2/3 cup milk
4 tbs. butter or margarine, melted and cooled
1-2 tbs. chopped nuts, optional
1-2 tbs. raisins, optional

Beat egg white in a small bowl until stiff and set aside. Mix together dry ingredients and set aside. Combine egg yolk, milk and butter. Add to dry ingredients, mixing until just blended. Add nuts and raisins if desired; fold in with beaten egg white until just mixed. Do not overbeat batter.

WHEAT FLAKE WAFFLES

3-4 waffles

Wheat flakes are similar in processing to oats. The flakes have a delicious, nutty flavor. In addition they retain much of the nutritional value of the wheat berry which is lost in the refining of the kernel to flour. Bake longer for a crispier waffle.

1 egg, room temperature and separated
3/4 cup whole wheat flour
3/4 cup wheat flakes
1 tsp. baking powder
1/8 tsp. salt
3/4 cup milk
1 tbs. honey
4 tbs. butter, melted and cooled

Beat egg white in a small bowl until stiff and set aside. Mix together dry ingredients and set aside. Combine egg yolk, milk, honey and melted butter. Add to dry ingredients, mixing until just blended. Fold in beaten egg white until just mixed. Do not overbeat batter.

GRANOLA WAFFLES

This wonderful waffle picks up the flavor and texture of your favorite granola.

1 egg, room temperature and separated
1 cup whole wheat or all purpose flour
3⁄4 cup granola cereal with or without dried fruits and nuts
1 tsp. baking powder
1⁄8 tsp. salt
1 tbs. honey
3⁄4 cup milk
4 tbs. butter or margarine, melted and cooled

Beat egg white in a small bowl until stiff and set aside. Mix together dry ingredients and set aside. Combine egg yolk, milk, honey, and melted butter. Add to dry ingredients, mixing until just blended. Fold in beaten egg white until just mixed. Do not overbeat batter.

OATMEAL WAFFLES

2 waffles

A must for oatmeal lovers. This is an extremely moist, incredibly good waffle. Better if cooked a little longer than normal for some crispiness.

1 egg, room temperature and separated
1½ cups oats
1 tsp. baking powder
⅛ tsp. salt
1 tbs. brown sugar
¾ cup milk
4 tbs. butter or margarine, melted and cooled

Beat egg white in a small bowl until stiff and set aside. Mix together dry ingredients and set aside. Combine egg yolk, milk and melted butter. Add to dry ingredients, mixing until just blended. Fold in beaten egg white until just mixed. Do not overbeat batter.

ANADAMA WAFFLES

A take-off on anadama bread, a favorite of many. A beautiful golden color — the wonderful combination of cornmeal and molasses makes this a true winner.

1 egg, room temperature and separated
3⁄4 cup all purpose flour
1⁄2 cup finely ground cornmeal
1 tsp. baking powder
1⁄8 tsp. salt
3⁄4 cup milk
1 tbs. molasses
4 tbs. butter or margarine, melted and cooled

Beat egg white in a small bowl until stiff and set aside. Mix together dry ingredients and set aside. Combine egg yolk, milk, molasses and butter. Add to dry ingredients, mixing until just blended. Fold in beaten egg white until just mixed. Do not overbeat batter.

Note: A coarsely ground cornmeal may make the waffles taste gritty.

CORN WAFFLES

3 waffles

For Southwestern flavor, top with with chili or salsa. For a Southern treat, serve with a creamed chicken topping.

1 egg, room temperature and separated
½ cup all purpose flour
½ cup cornmeal
1 tsp. baking powder
⅛ tsp. salt
¾ cup milk
½ cup corn kernels (I used drained, canned corn)
1 tbs. honey
4 tbs. butter or margarine, melted and cooled

Beat egg white in a small bowl until stiff and set aside. Mix together dry ingredients and set aside. Combine egg yolk, milk, corn, honey and butter. Add to dry ingredients, mixing until just blended. Fold in beaten egg white until just mixed. Do not overbeat batter.

OAT BRAN WAFFLES

Tasty and so nutritional too!

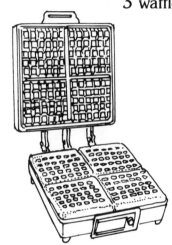

1 egg, room temperature and separated
1/2 cup all purpose flour
1/2 cup oats (quick cooking or regular)
1/2 cup oat bran (wheat or rice bran may also be used)
1 tsp. baking powder
1/8 tsp. salt
3/4 cup milk
1 tbs. honey
4 tbs. butter or margarine, melted and cooled

Beat egg white in a small bowl until stiff and set aside. Mix together dry ingredients and set aside. Combine egg yolk, milk, honey and butter. Add to dry ingredients, mixing until just blended. Fold in beaten egg white until just mixed. Do not overbeat batter.

BUCKWHEAT WAFFLES

Buckwheat is a strong tasting flour which is why such a small amount is used. One of the most common uses of the flour is for pancakes and waffles.

1 egg, room temperature and separated
1 cup all purpose flour
¼ cup buckwheat flour
1 tsp. baking powder
⅛ tsp. salt
¾ cup milk
1 tbs. honey
4 tbs. butter or margarine, melted and cooled

Beat egg white in a small bowl until stiff and set aside. Mix together dry ingredients and set aside. Combine egg yolk, milk, honey and butter. Add to dry ingredients, mixing until just blended. Fold in beaten egg white until just mixed. Do not overbeat batter.

Note: Try using any of these or your favorite flours which have high nutritional contents: quinoa, amaranth, teff, flaxseed.

BANANA BRAN WAFFLES

This delightful, flavorful waffle has the nutritional benefits of bran.

1 egg, room temperature and separated
½ cup all purpose flour
¼ cup oats (quick cooking or regular)
¼ cup bran (oat, wheat or rice)
1 tsp. baking powder
⅛ tsp. salt
1 tbs. brown sugar
½ cup milk
1 medium banana, mashed
4 tbs. butter or margarine melted and cooled
2-3 tbs. chopped nuts, optional

Beat egg white in a small bowl until stiff and set aside. Mix together dry ingredients and set aside. Combine egg yolk, milk, banana and butter. Add to dry ingredients, mixing until just blended. Add nuts and fold in with beaten egg white until just mixed. Do not overbeat batter.

WILD RICE WAFFLES

3 waffles

Wild rice waffles are very light and crispy. The wild rice gives these waffles a smokey, nutty taste.

1 egg, room temperature and separated
1¼ cups all purpose flour
½ cup cooked wild rice
1 tsp. baking powder
⅛ tsp. salt
1 tbs. brown sugar
¾ cup milk
4 tbs. butter or margarine, melted and cooled

Beat egg white in a small bowl until stiff and set aside. Mix together dry ingredients and set aside. Combine egg yolk, milk and butter. Add to dry ingredients, mixing until just blended. Fold in beaten egg white until just mixed. Do not overbeat batter.

RICE WAFFLES

If you like the taste and texture of rice you'll enjoy this light waffle.

1 egg, room temperature and separated
1 cup all purpose flour
3/4 cup cooked rice
1 tsp. baking powder
1/8 tsp. salt
1 tbs. sugar (white or brown)
3/4 cup milk
4 tbs. butter or margarine, melted and cooled

Beat egg white in a small bowl until stiff and set aside. Mix together dry ingredients and set aside. Combine egg yolk, milk and butter. Add to dry ingredients, mixing until just blended. Fold in rice and beaten egg white until just mixed. Do not overbeat batter.

Variation: COCONUT RICE WAFFLES

Substitute coconut cream (canned) for the regular milk and add 2 tbs. of coconut flakes.

RYE WAFFLES

3 waffles

The taste is a real surprise unless you know it's coming! A must for rye lovers.

1 egg, room temperature and separated
½ cup all purpose flour
½ cup rye flour
1 tsp. baking powder
⅛ tsp. salt
1 tsp. caraway seeds, or to taste
¾ cup milk
1 tbs. honey
4 tbs. butter or margarine, melted and cooled

Beat egg white in a small bowl until stiff and set aside. Mix together dry ingredients and set aside. Combine egg yolk, milk, honey and butter. Add to dry ingredients, mixing until just blended. Fold in beaten egg white until just mixed. Do not overbeat batter.

SCANDINAVIAN RYE WAFFLES

3 waffles

The various seeds really perk up the flavor of these waffles.

1 egg, room temperature and separated
½ cup all purpose flour
½ cup rye flour
1 tsp. baking powder
⅛ tsp. salt
¼ tsp. orange peel
½ tsp. caraway seeds
½ tsp. fennel seeds
¾ cup milk
1 tbs. molasses
4 tbs. butter or margarine, melted and cooled

Beat egg white in a small bowl until stiff and set aside. Mix together dry ingredients and set aside. Combine egg yolk, milk, molasses and butter. Add to dry ingredients, mixing until just blended. Fold in beaten egg white until just mixed. Do not overbeat batter.

SPICE WAFFLES

*A great change-of-pace waffle, perfect for a cold, raining, lazy day. Serve with apple butter, **Sautéed Apples**, page 146, or applesauce (warm in microwave if desired).*

1 egg, room temperature and separated	1/8 tsp. ground cloves
1 cup all purpose flour	1/2 tsp. cinnamon
1 tsp. baking powder	1/16 tsp. nutmeg
1/8 tsp. salt	3/4 cup milk
1 tbs. brown sugar	4 tbs. butter or margarine, melted and cooled

Beat egg white in a small bowl until stiff and set aside. Mix together dry ingredients and set aside. Combine egg yolk, milk and butter. Add to dry ingredients, mixing until just blended. Fold in beaten egg white until just mixed. Do not overbeat batter.

Variation: SPICED APPLE WAFFLES
Add 1/4 medium apple, peeled and diced, and 2-3 tbs. chopped walnuts. Fold both in with the egg white.

SAFFRON WAFFLES

Saffron is one of the world's most expensive spices, but only the smallest amount is used to achieve the wonderful color and taste in these waffles.

1 egg, room temperature and separated
1 cup all purpose flour
1 tsp. baking powder
1/8 tsp. salt
1 tbs. sugar
1/8 tsp. saffron threads or 1/16 tsp. powdered saffron
1/8 tsp. nutmeg
3/4 cup milk
4 tbs. butter or margarine, melted and cooled
2-3 tbs. raisins, optional

Beat egg white in a small bowl until stiff and set aside. Mix together dry ingredients and set aside. Combine egg yolk, milk and butter. Add to dry ingredients, mixing until just blended. Add raisins if desired and fold in with beaten egg white until just mixed. Do not overbeat batter.

ANISE WAFFLES

For a true Middle Eastern flavor, add the sesame seeds to the batter or sprinkle on top prior to baking. A delightful taste with a light, but crispy texture.

1 egg, room temperature and separated
1 cup all purpose flour
1 tsp. baking powder
⅛ tsp. salt
2 tbs. sugar
1 tsp. anise seed, or to taste
1 tsp. sesame seeds, optional
¾ cup milk
4 tbs. butter or margarine, melted and cooled

Beat egg white in a small bowl until stiff and set aside. Mix together dry ingredients and set aside. Combine egg yolk, milk and butter. Add to dry ingredients, mixing until just blended. Fold in beaten egg white until just mixed. Do not overbeat batter.

POPPY SEED WAFFLES

Poppy seeds give a sweet, delicate taste to this waffle.

1 egg, room temperature and separated
1 cup all purpose flour
1 tsp. baking powder
⅛ tsp. salt
1 tbs. sugar
2 tsp.-1 tbs. poppy seeds, or to taste
¾ cup milk
1 tsp. almond extract
4 tbs. butter or margarine, melted and cooled

Beat egg white in a small bowl until stiff and set aside. Mix together dry ingredients and set aside. Combine egg yolk, milk, almond extract and melted butter. Add to dry ingredients, mixing until just blended. Fold in beaten egg white until just mixed. Do not overbeat batter.

VANILLA WAFFLES

3 waffles

This recipe makes a light batter and waffle with wonderful vanilla flavor. For best results, use real vanilla instead of imitation.

1 egg, room temperature and separated
1 cup all purpose flour
1 tsp. baking powder
1/8 tsp. salt
1 tbs. brown sugar
3/4 cup milk
1 tbs. vanilla extract
3 tbs. butter or margarine, melted and cooled

Beat egg white in a small bowl until stiff and set aside. Mix together dry ingredients and set aside. Combine egg yolk, milk, vanilla and butter. Add to dry ingredients, mixing until just blended. Fold in beaten egg white until just mixed. Do not overbeat batter.

CRYSTALLIZED GINGER WAFFLES 3 waffles

Wow! You're going to love this! Crystallized ginger is pieces of ginger root which have been candied and sugared. Jars or boxes of crystallized or candied ginger may be found in a well-stocked spice section of your grocery, wherever Chinese groceries are sold, in gourmet shops or by mail order. When the ginger is chopped (with your food processor or blender) it becomes soft and pliable.

1 egg, room temperature and
  separated
1¼ cups all purpose flour
1 tsp. baking powder
1 tbs. brown sugar
¾ cup milk
1 tbs. vanilla extract (not imitation)

1 tsp. chopped crystallized ginger,
  or to taste
4 tbs. butter or margarine, melted
  and cooled
¼ cup chopped nuts (walnuts,
  pecans or macadamias)
¼ cup chocolate chips

Beat egg white in a small bowl until stiff and set aside. Mix together dry ingredients and set aside. Combine egg yolk, milk, vanilla, ginger and butter. Add to dry ingredients, mixing until just blended. Add nuts and chocolate chips; fold in with beaten egg white until just mixed. Do not overbeat batter.

CARAWAY WAFFLES

Many people equate caraway with rye — until it's eaten with a basic waffle like this!

1 egg, room temperature and separated
1 cup all purpose flour
1 tsp. baking powder
⅛ tsp. salt
1½ tsp. caraway seeds, or to taste
¾ cup milk
1 tbs. honey
4 tbs. butter or margarine, melted and cooled

Beat egg white in a small bowl until stiff and set aside. Mix together dry ingredients and set aside. Combine egg yolk, milk, honey and butter. Add to dry ingredients, mixing until just blended. Fold in beaten egg white until just mixed. Do not overbeat batter.

CARDAMOM WAFFLES

A very distinctive taste - cardamom is commonly used in Scandinavian sweets and breads. Look for it in well-stocked grocery stores or gourmet shops.

1 egg, room temperature and separated
1¼ cups all purpose flour
1 tsp. baking powder
⅛ tsp. salt
⅛ tsp. orange peel
⅛ tsp. lemon peel
¼ tsp. cardamom
¾ cup milk
1 tbs. honey
4 tbs. butter or margarine, melted and cooled

Beat egg white in a small bowl until stiff and set aside. Mix together dry ingredients and set aside. Combine egg yolk, milk, honey and butter. Add to dry ingredients, mixing until just blended. Fold in beaten egg white until just mixed. Do not overbeat batter.

FRUIT WAFFLES

Note: See *Nut and Nut Butter Waffles*, page 109, for additional waffles which include fruits.

APPLE WAFFLES

A delicate taste of apples gives these waffles an uplifting flavor.

1 egg, room temperature and separated
1 cup all purpose flour
1 tsp. baking powder
⅛ tsp. salt
⅛ tsp. cinnamon
1 tbs. sugar
⅔ cup apple juice
4 tbs. butter or margarine, melted and cooled
¼ medium apple, peeled and diced

Beat egg white in a small bowl until stiff and set aside. Mix together dry ingredients and set aside. Combine egg yolk, juice and melted butter. Add to dry ingredients, mixing until just blended. Add diced apple and fold in with beaten egg white until just mixed. Do not overbeat batter.

BANANA WAFFLES

A superb banana waffle with lots of that favorite banana flavor. Very moist.

1 egg, room temperature and separated
1 cup all purpose flour
1 tsp. baking powder
⅛ tsp. salt
1 tbs. sugar
½ cup milk
1 cup mashed banana (about 2 medium, well ripened bananas)
4 tbs. butter or margarine, melted and cooled
2-3 tbs. chopped nuts (walnuts or pecans)

Beat egg white in a small bowl until stiff and set aside. Mix together dry ingredients and set aside. Combine egg yolk, milk, banana and melted butter. Add to dry ingredients, mixing until just blended. Add nuts and fold in with beaten egg white until just mixed. Do not overbeat batter.

STRAWBERRY WAFFLES

Who doesn't love hot waffles served with a favorite berry? Bake the berry into the waffle itself for a truly wonderful breakfast treat. Serve them as a dessert with ice cream. Raspberries, blackberries, blueberries, or other berries may also be used.

1 egg, room temperature and separated
1 cup all purpose flour
1 tsp. baking powder
⅛ tsp. salt
⅓ cup milk
1 tbs. honey or strawberry (or other berry) syrup
½ cup pureed strawberries (fresh or thawed frozen)
3 tbs. butter or margarine, melted and cooled
¼-⅓ cup chopped nuts, optional

Beat egg white in a small bowl until stiff and set aside. Mix together dry ingredients and set aside. Combine egg yolk, milk, honey or syrup, strawberries and melted butter. Add to dry ingredients, mixing until just blended. Add nuts, if desired, and fold in with beaten egg white until just mixed. Do not overbeat batter.

HAWAIIAN WAFFLES

This is a treat for breakfast or dessert.

1 egg, room temperature and separated
¾ cup all purpose flour
½ cup oatmeal
1 tsp. baking powder
⅛ tsp. salt
1 tbs. brown sugar
2 tbs. coconut flakes
¾ cup Mauna Lai (or similar juice), or milk
4 tbs. butter, melted and cooled to warm
1-2 tbs. chocolate chips
1-2 tbs. chopped macadamia nuts

Beat egg white in a small bowl until stiff and set aside. Mix together dry ingredients and set aside. Combine egg yolk, juice or milk and melted butter. Add to dry ingredients, mixing until just blended. Add chocolate chips and nuts. Fold in with beaten egg white until just mixed. Do not overbeat batter.

CRANBERRY PINEAPPLE WAFFLES

Here is a delightful treat for Thanksgiving or any fall morning.

1 egg, room temperature and separated
1 cup all purpose flour
1 tsp. baking powder
1/8 tsp. salt
1 tbs. brown sugar
2/3 cup pineapple or cranberry juice
1/4 cup crushed pineapple, drained
1/4 cup chopped cranberries
4 tbs. butter, melted and cooled
2-3 tbs. chopped pecans or walnuts, optional

Beat egg white in a small bowl until stiff and set aside. Mix together dry ingredients and set aside. Combine egg yolk, juice, pineapple, cranberries and melted butter. Add to dry ingredients, mixing until just blended. Add nuts, if desired, and fold in with beaten egg white until just mixed. Do not overbeat batter.

COCONUT PINEAPPLE WAFFLES

Try this delightful tropical waffle.

1 egg, room temperature and separated
1 cup all purpose flour
1 tsp. baking powder
⅛ tsp. salt
1 tbs. brown sugar
2 tbs. coconut flakes
½ cup pineapple juice
¼ cup crushed pineapple, well drained (canned)
4 tbs. butter or margarine, melted and cooled

Beat egg white in a small bowl until stiff and set aside. Mix together dry ingredients and set aside. Combine egg yolk, juice, pineapple and melted butter. Add to dry ingredients, mixing until just blended. Fold in beaten egg white until just mixed. Do not overbeat batter.

ORANGE BANANA WAFFLES

A favorite combination which is sure to be a winner.

1 egg, room temperature and separated
1 cup all purpose flour
1 tsp. baking powder
⅛ tsp. salt
1 tbs. sugar
½ cup orange juice
⅓ cup mashed banana
4 tbs. butter or margarine, melted and cooled

Beat egg white in a small bowl until stiff and set aside. Mix together dry ingredients and set aside. Combine egg yolk, juice, banana and melted butter. Add to dry ingredients, mixing until just blended. Fold in beaten egg white until just mixed. Do not overbeat batter.

STRAWBERRY BANANA WAFFLES

What a combination! Sure to please. The batter is somewhat thicker than normal.

1 egg, room temperature and separated
1 tsp. baking powder
1 cup all purpose flour
1/8 tsp. salt
1/4 cup milk
1 tbs. strawberry syrup or honey
1/4 cup pureed strawberries
1/4 cup mashed bananas
4 tbs. butter or margarine, melted and cooled

Beat egg white in a small bowl until stiff and set aside. Mix together dry ingredients and set aside. Combine egg yolk, milk, syrup or honey, strawberries, banana and melted butter. Add to dry ingredients, mixing until just blended. Fold in beaten egg white until just mixed. Do not overbeat batter.

PEACH WAFFLES

You'll enjoy the delicate peach flavoring. Serve with **Peach and Orange Syrup,** *page 150, for a tasty delight.*

1 egg, room temperature and
  separated
1 cup all purpose flour
1 tsp. baking powder
1/8 tsp. salt

2 tsp. brown sugar
1/8 tsp. cinnamon
1 cup peach puree
4 tbs. butter or margarine, melted
  and cooled

Beat egg white in a small bowl until stiff and set aside. Mix together dry ingredients and set aside. Combine egg yolk, peach puree and melted butter. Add to dry ingredients, mixing until just blended. Fold in beaten egg white until just mixed. Do not overbeat batter.

NOTE: Puree peeled fresh or rinsed canned peaches in a food processor.

Variation: APPLE OR PEAR WAFFLES
Substitute apple or pear puree for the peach puree. Fresh apples or pears should be cooked in almost boiling water until soft prior to pureeing.

BANANA, COCONUT AND MACADAMIA WAFFLES

Out of this world. Three different tastes blend into one.

1 egg, room temperature and separated
1 cup all purpose flour
1 tsp. baking powder
1/8 tsp. salt
1 tsp. brown sugar
2 tbs. coconut flakes
1/2 cup coconut (canned) or regular milk
1/2 cup mashed banana
1 tsp. coconut extract (vanilla may be substituted)
4 tbs. butter or margarine, melted and cooled
1/4-1/3 cup chopped macadamias, or walnuts

Beat egg white in a small bowl until stiff and set aside. Mix together dry ingredients and set aside. Combine egg yolk, coconut milk, banana, coconut extract and melted butter. Add to dry ingredients, mixing until just blended. Add nuts and fold in with beaten egg white until just mixed. Do not overbeat batter.

ORANGE CINNAMON OATMEAL WAFFLES   3 waffles

This delicious oatmeal waffle has a great orange flavor.

1 egg, room temperature and separated
½ cup all purpose flour
1 cup oats
1 tsp. baking powder
⅛ tsp. salt
1 tbs. brown sugar
½ tsp. cinnamon
⅛ tsp. orange peel
¾ cup orange juice
4 tbs. butter or margarine, melted and cooled
¼ cup chopped walnuts, optional

Beat egg white in a small bowl until stiff and set aside. Mix together dry ingredients and set aside. Combine egg yolk, juice and butter. Add to dry ingredients, mixing until just blended. Add nuts, if desired, and fold in with beaten egg white until just mixed. Do not overbeat batter.

CRANBERRY WAFFLES

*This tangy waffle is great served with **Cranberry Butter**, page 144.*

1 egg, room temperature and separated
1 cup all purpose flour
1 tsp. baking powder
1/8 tsp. salt
3/4 cup cranberry juice
2-3 tbs. chopped fresh cranberries, or to taste
1 tbs. honey
3 tbs. butter or margarine, melted and cooled

Beat egg white in a small bowl until stiff and set aside. Mix together dry ingredients and set aside. Combine egg yolk, juice, cranberries, honey and butter. Add to dry ingredients, mixing until just blended. Fold in beaten egg white until just mixed. Do not overbeat batter.

PEANUT BUTTER DATE WAFFLES

3 waffles

The taste of peanut butter and dates combine beautifully to flavor this outstanding waffle.

1 egg, room temperature and separated
1 cup all purpose flour
1 tsp. baking powder
1/8 tsp. salt
2/3 cup milk
1/4 cup peanut butter
1 tbs. honey
2 tbs. butter or margarine, melted and cooled to warm (not hot)
1/4 cup chopped dates

Beat egg white in a small bowl until stiff and set aside. Mix together dry ingredients and set aside. Combine egg yolk, milk, peanut butter, honey and butter. Add to dry ingredients, mixing until just blended. Mix in dates and fold in with beaten egg white until just mixed. Do not overbeat batter.

CRAN-ORANGE WAFFLES

3 waffles

The dried cranberries, which add lots of zest to these waffles, may be found in some large grocery stores, gourmet shops or by mail order. Use in place of raisins in any of your favorite recipes for a change-of-pace treat.

1 egg, room temperature and separated
1 cup all purpose flour
1 tsp. baking powder
1/8 tsp. salt
1 tbs. brown sugar
1 tsp. orange peel
1/4 cup milk
1/2 cup orange juice
4 tbs. butter or margarine, melted and cooled
1/4-1/3 cup dried cranberries

Beat egg white in a small bowl until stiff and set aside. Mix together dry ingredients and set aside. Combine egg yolk, milk, juice and butter. Add to dry ingredients, mixing until just blended. Add cranberries and fold in with beaten egg white until just mixed. Do not overbeat batter.

APPLE CIDER WAFFLES

The orange peel is the secret ingredient which makes these waffles surprise you with an unexpected taste.

1 egg, room temperature and separated
1 cup all purpose flour
1 tsp. baking powder
1/8 tsp. salt
1 tbs. brown sugar
1/4 tsp. orange peel
2/3 cup apple cider, or apple juice
1/4 medium apple, peeled and diced
4 tbs. butter or margarine, melted and cooled

Beat egg white in a small bowl until stiff and set aside. Mix together dry ingredients and set aside. Combine egg yolk, cider, apple and butter. Add to dry ingredients, mixing until just blended. Fold in beaten egg white until just mixed. Do not overbeat batter.

APPLE OATMEAL WAFFLES

One of the best. Do not overcook.

1 egg, room temperature and separated
¾ cup all purpose flour
¾ cup oats
1 tsp. baking powder
⅛ tsp. salt
½ tsp. cinnamon
¾ cup apple juice
1 tbs. honey
4 tbs. butter or margarine, melted and cooled
¼ medium apple, peeled and diced, or 1-2 tbs. diced dried apples
¼ cup chopped walnuts, optional
2 tbs. raisins, optional

Beat egg white in a small bowl until stiff and set aside. Mix together dry ingredients and set aside. Combine egg yolk, juice, honey and butter. Add to dry ingredients, mixing until just blended. Add apple, nuts and raisins; fold in with beaten egg white until just mixed. Do not overbeat batter.

APPLE CARROT WAFFLES

An absolutely delightful combination.

1 egg, room temperature and separated
1 cup all purpose flour
1 tsp. baking powder
1/8 tsp. salt
1/8 tsp. cinnamon
1 tbs. brown sugar
2/3 cup apple juice
1/4 cup grated carrots
1/4 apple, peeled and finely diced
4 tbs. butter or margarine, melted and cooled
2-3 tbs. raisins, optional
2-3 tbs. chopped walnuts, optional

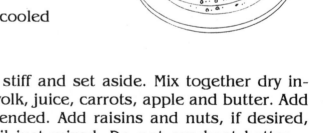

Beat egg white in a small bowl until stiff and set aside. Mix together dry ingredients and set aside. Combine egg yolk, juice, carrots, apple and butter. Add to dry ingredients, mixing until just blended. Add raisins and nuts, if desired, and fold in with beaten egg white until just mixed. Do not overbeat batter.

CARROT, CHERRIES AND COCONUT WAFFLES

A cake-like waffle, this doesn't even need syrup! (Of course syrup may ALWAYS be used.)

1 egg, room temperature and
  separated
1 cup all purpose flour
1 tsp. baking powder
⅛ tsp. salt
1 tsp. sugar
⅛ tsp. cinnamon
1 tbs. flaked coconut

¾ cup coconut milk (canned)
¼ cup grated carrots
6 maraschino cherries, halved
  or quartered
4 tbs. butter or margarine, melted
  and cooled
¼-⅓ cup chopped walnuts

Beat egg white in a small bowl until stiff and set aside. Mix together dry ingredients and set aside. Combine egg yolk, coconut milk, carrots, cherries and butter. Add to dry ingredients, mixing until just blended. Add nuts and fold in with beaten egg white until just mixed. Do not overbeat batter.

PEANUT BUTTER BANANA WAFFLES

3 waffles

*The batter is relatively thick. A great taste combination of peanut butter and banana. Top with **Peanut Butter Honey,** page 149.*

1 egg, room temperature and separated
1 cup all purpose flour
1 tsp. baking powder
⅛ tsp. salt
1 medium banana, mashed
½ cup milk
⅓ cup peanut butter
1 tbs. honey
2 tbs. butter or margarine, melted and cooled

Beat egg white in a small bowl until stiff and set aside. Mix together dry ingredients and set aside. Combine egg yolk, banana, milk, peanut butter, honey and butter. Add to dry ingredients, mixing until just blended. Fold in beaten egg white until just mixed. Do not overbeat batter.

MINTED APPLE WAFFLES

A great minty apple - superb with fresh mint if you have it.

1 egg, room temperature and separated
1 cup all purpose flour
1 tsp. baking powder
1/8 tsp. salt
1 tbs. sugar
1/2 tsp. dried mint, or 1 1/2 tsp. chopped fresh
2/3 cup apple juice
1/4 medium apple, peeled and diced
1/2 tsp. mint extract
4 tbs. butter or margarine, melted and cooled

Beat egg white in a small bowl until stiff and set aside. Mix together dry ingredients and set aside. Combine egg yolk, juice, apple, extract and butter. Add to dry ingredients, mixing until just blended. Fold in beaten egg white until just mixed. Do not overbeat batter.

CRAN-FRUIT WAFFLES

3 waffles

Enjoy the great taste of cranberry waffles without having to chop the cranberries or when they are not in season. Cran-Fruit is a combination of cranberry sauce and other fruits, and is usually found with canned fruit products in your grocery store.

1 egg, room temperature and separated
1⅓ cups all purpose flour
1 tsp. baking powder
⅛ tsp. salt
⅔ cup milk
⅓ cup Cran-Fruit
1 tbs. honey
4 tbs. butter or margarine, melted and cooled
¼ chopped walnuts or pecans, optional

Beat egg white in a small bowl until stiff and set aside. Mix together dry ingredients and set aside. Combine egg yolk, milk, Cran-Fruit, honey and butter. Add to dry ingredients, mixing until just blended. Add nuts, if desired, and fold in with beaten egg white until just mixed. Do not overbeat batter.

PINEAPPLE STRAWBERRY WAFFLES

3 waffles

A moist, unique, flavorful waffle.

1 egg, room temperature and separated
1 cup all purpose flour
1 tsp. baking powder
⅛ tsp. salt
1 tbs. sugar
½ cup strawberries, pureed
¼ cup pineapple juice
¼ cup crushed pineapple, drained
4 tbs. butter or margarine, melted and cooled

Beat egg white in a small bowl until stiff and set aside. Mix together dry ingredients and set aside. Combine egg yolk, strawberries, juice, pineapple and butter. Add to dry ingredients, mixing until just blended. Fold in beaten egg white until just mixed. Do not overbeat batter.

GRAPE APPLE WAFFLES

3 waffles

A delicate, flavorful waffle.

1 egg, room temperature and separated
1¼ cups all purpose flour
1 tsp. baking powder
⅛ tsp. salt
1 tbs. sugar
½ tsp. lemon peel
¾ cup white grape juice
4 tbs. butter or margarine, melted and cooled
¼ medium apple, peeled and diced, or pear

Beat egg white in a small bowl until stiff and set aside. Mix together dry ingredients and set aside. Combine egg yolk, juice, apple and butter. Add to dry ingredients, mixing until just blended. Fold in beaten egg white until just mixed. Do not overbeat batter.

GRAPE ORANGE WAFFLES

A wonderful combination.

1 egg, room temperature and separated
1 cup all purpose flour
1 tsp. baking powder
1/8 tsp. salt
1 tbs. sugar
1/2 cup white grape juice
1/2 cup mandarin orange segments
4 tbs. butter or margarine, melted and cooled
1/4 tsp. orange peel

Beat egg white in a small bowl until stiff and set aside. Mix together dry ingredients and set aside. Combine egg yolk, juice, orange segments and butter. Add to dry ingredients, mixing until just blended. Fold in beaten egg white until just mixed. Do not overbeat batter.

Note: The mandarin orange segments will become somewhat crushed during the mixing, which adds liquid to the batter but you will also have orange chunks in the waffles, adding a nice texture.

CITRUS PINEAPPLE WAFFLES

This moist waffle has lots of fruity flavor.

1 egg, room temperature and separated
1 cup all purpose flour
1 tsp. baking powder
1/8 tsp. salt
1 tbs. sugar
1/4 tsp. orange peel
1/3 cup grapefruit juice
1/3 cup orange juice
1/4 cup crushed pineapple, drained
4 tbs. butter or margarine, melted and cooled

Beat egg white in a small bowl until stiff and set aside. Mix together dry ingredients and set aside. Combine egg yolk, juices, pineapple and butter. Add to dry ingredients, mixing until just blended. Fold in beaten egg white until just mixed. Do not overbeat batter.

PINEAPPLE, CHERRIES AND ORANGE WAFFLES

The cherries make these waffles very festive looking as well as tasty.

1 egg, room temperature and separated
1 cup all purpose flour
1 tsp. baking powder
⅛ tsp. salt
1 tbs. sugar
⅛ tsp. orange peel
½ cup pineapple juice
¼ cup maraschino cherries
¼ cup mandarin orange segments
4 tbs. butter or margarine, melted and cooled

Beat egg white in a small bowl until stiff and set aside. Mix together dry ingredients and set aside. Combine egg yolk, juice, cherries, orange segments and butter. Add to dry ingredients, mixing until just blended. Fold in beaten egg white until just mixed. Do not overbeat batter.

PINEAPPLE PAPAYA WAFFLES

3 waffles

What a combination! You'll love it.

1 egg, room temperature and separated
1 cup all purpose flour
1 tsp. baking powder
⅛ tsp. salt
1 tbs. sugar
½ cup pineapple juice
¼ cup papaya juice
4 tbs. butter or margarine, melted and cooled

Beat egg white in a small bowl until stiff and set aside. Mix together dry ingredients and set aside. Combine egg yolk, juices, and butter. Add to dry ingredients, mixing until just blended. Fold in beaten egg white until just mixed. Do not overbeat batter.

CRANAPPLE WAFFLES

The small pieces of apple and cranberry lend lots of great texture and taste to this distinctive waffle. A favorite combination.

1 egg, room temperature and separated
1 cup all purpose flour
1 tsp. baking powder
⅛ tsp. salt
1 tbs. sugar
⅛ tsp. cinnamon
⅔ cup cranapple, cranberry, or apple juice
¼ medium apple, peeled and diced
¼ cup chopped cranberries
4 tbs. butter or margarine, melted and cooled
2-3 tbs. chopped nuts, optional

Beat egg white in a small bowl until stiff and set aside. Mix together dry ingredients and set aside. Combine egg yolk, juice, apple, cranberries and butter. Add to dry ingredients, mixing until just blended. Add nuts and fold in with beaten egg white until just mixed. Do not overbeat batter.

CRANAPPLE PINEAPPLE WAFFLES

3 waffles

Medium thick batter with chunks of fruit make for delicious waffles. Cook a little longer than normal for a crispier waffle.

1 egg, room temperature and separated
1 cup all purpose flour
1 tsp. baking powder
⅛ tsp. salt
1 tbs. sugar
½ cup cranapple, cranberry, apple or pineapple juice
¼ medium apple, peeled and diced
¼ cup chopped cranberries
¼ cup crushed pineapple, drained
4 tbs. butter or margarine, melted and cooled
2-3 tbs. chopped nuts, optional

Beat egg white in a small bowl until stiff and set aside. Mix together dry ingredients and set aside. Combine egg yolk, juice, apple, cranberries, pineapple and butter. Add to dry ingredients, mixing until just blended. Add nuts and fold in with beaten egg white until just mixed. Do not overbeat batter.

BANANA PINEAPPLE WAFFLES

3 waffles

A tropical island delight.

1 egg, room temperature and separated
1 cup all purpose flour
1 tsp. baking powder
1/8 tsp. salt
1 tbs. sugar
1/2 cup pineapple juice
1/4 cup crushed pineapple, drained
1/2 cup mashed banana (about one medium banana)
4 tbs. butter or margarine, melted and cooled
2-3 tbs. chopped macadamias or walnuts, optional

Beat egg white in a small bowl until stiff and set aside. Mix together dry ingredients and set aside. Combine egg yolk, juice, pineapple, banana and butter. Add to dry ingredients, mixing until just blended. Add nuts, if desired, and fold in with beaten egg white until just mixed. Do not overbeat batter.

ORANGE APPLE WAFFLES

You'll love this one!

1 egg, room temperature and separated
1 cup all purpose flour
1 tsp. baking powder
⅛ tsp. salt
1 tbs. sugar
¼ tsp. orange peel
½ cup apple juice
½ cup mandarin orange segments
4 tbs. butter or margarine, melted and cooled

Beat egg white in a small bowl until stiff and set aside. Mix together dry ingredients and set aside. Combine egg yolk, juice, orange segments and butter. Add to dry ingredients, mixing until just blended. Fold in beaten egg white until just mixed. Do not overbeat batter.

PINEAPPLE, STRAWBERRY AND BANANA WAFFLES

Here's another wonderful, fruity waffle that you're going to love.

1 egg, room temperature and separated
1 cup all purpose flour
1 tsp. baking powder
⅛ tsp. salt
1 tbs. sugar
1 medium banana, mashed
¼ cup strawberry puree
¼ cup pineapple juice
4 tbs. butter or margarine, melted and cooled

Beat egg white in a small bowl until stiff and set aside. Mix together dry ingredients and set aside. Combine egg yolk, banana, strawberry puree, juice and butter. Add to dry ingredients, mixing until just blended. Fold in beaten egg white until just mixed. Do not overbeat batter.

PINEAPPLE ORANGE MINT WAFFLES

3 waffles

The aroma of mint will have people standing in line for these waffles.

1 egg, room temperature and separated
1 cup all purpose flour
1 tsp. baking powder
1/8 tsp. salt
1 tbs. sugar
1/4 tsp. dried mint leaves or 3/4 tsp. fresh crushed leaves
2/3 cup orange juice
1/4 cup crushed pineapple, drained
1/2 tsp. mint extract
4 tbs. butter or margarine, melted and cooled

Beat egg white in a small bowl until stiff and set aside. Mix together dry ingredients and set aside. Combine egg yolk, juice, pineapple, mint extract and butter. Add to dry ingredients, mixing until just blended. Fold in beaten egg white until just mixed. Do not overbeat batter.

APPLE, PEACH AND CARROT WAFFLES

3 waffles

Peaple will ask about the secret ingredients in this interesting waffle. Sure to please.

1 egg, room temperature and separated
1 cup all purpose flour
1 tsp. baking powder
⅛ tsp. salt
1 tbs. sugar
⅛ tsp. cinnamon
¾ cup apple juice
¼ cup grated carrots
2-3 tbs. dried peaches, diced
4 tbs. butter or margarine, melted and cooled

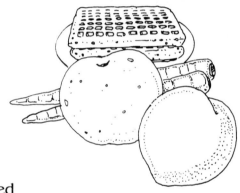

Beat egg white in a small bowl until stiff and set aside. Mix together dry ingredients and set aside. Combine egg yolk, juice, carrots, peaches and butter. Add to dry ingredients, mixing until just blended. Fold in beaten egg white until just mixed. Do not overbeat batter.

WEST INDIES BANANA WAFFLES

A truly irresistible, sweet waffle. This is one of our absolute favorites.

1 egg, room temperature and separated
1 cup all purpose flour
1 tsp. baking powder
⅛ tsp. salt
1 tbs. sugar
¼ tsp. cinnamon
⅛ tsp. nutmeg
½ cup coconut milk (canned)
1 medium banana, mashed
1 tsp. coconut extract
4 tbs. butter or margarine, melted and cooled
1 tbs. coconut flakes

Beat egg white in a small bowl until stiff and set aside. Mix together dry ingredients and set aside. Combine egg yolk, milk, banana, coconut extract and butter. Add to dry ingredients, mixing until just blended. Fold in beaten egg white until just mixed. Do not overbeat batter.

PUMPKIN WAFFLES

2 waffles

A wonderful flavorful pumpkin treat. Best if cooked longer so it's nice and crispy.

1 egg, room temperature and separated
½ cup all purpose flour
¾ cup oats (regular or quick cooking)
1 tsp. baking powder
⅛ tsp. salt
1 tbs. brown sugar
¼ tsp. pumpkin pie spice
⅓ cup milk
½ cup canned or cooked, pureed pumpkin
4 tbs. butter or margarine, melted and cooled
¼ cup chopped walnuts or pecans, optional

Beat egg white in a small bowl until stiff and set aside. Mix together dry ingredients and set aside. Combine egg yolk, milk, pumpkin and butter. Add to dry ingredients, mixing until just blended. Add nuts and fold in with beaten egg white until just mixed. Do not overbeat batter.

CINNAMON RAISIN WAFFLES

You'll absolutely love this from the first bite. Light and crispy.

1 egg, room temperature and separated
1¼ cups all purpose flour
1 tsp. baking powder
⅛ tsp. salt
1 tbs. brown sugar
½ tsp. cinnamon
¾ cup milk
4 tbs. butter or margarine, melted and cooled
¼-⅓ cup raisins
¼ cup chopped walnuts or pecans, optional

Beat egg white in a small bowl until stiff and set aside. Mix together dry ingredients and set aside. Combine egg yolk, milk and butter. Add to dry ingredients, mixing until just blended. Add nuts, if desired, and fold in with beaten egg white until just mixed. Do not overbeat batter.

MAPLE BANANA WAFFLES

This is an incredibly moist waffle. It may be baked longer for added crispiness, if desired.

1 egg, room temperature and separated
1 cup all purpose flour
1 tsp. baking powder
⅛ tsp. salt
½ cup milk
2 medium bananas, mashed
2 tbs. maple syrup
4 tbs. butter or margarine, melted and cooled
2-3 tbs. chopped nuts, optional

Beat egg white in a small bowl until stiff and set aside. Mix together dry ingredients and set aside. Combine egg yolk, milk, banana, syrup and butter. Add to dry ingredients, mixing until just blended. Add nuts, if desired, and fold in with beaten egg white until just mixed. Do not overbeat batter.

BANANA PAPAYA WAFFLES

A moist waffle with a wonderful tropical flavor.

1 egg, room temperature and separated
1 cup all purpose flour
1 tsp. baking powder
⅛ tsp. salt
2 tsp. brown sugar
¾ cup papaya juice
1 medium banana, mashed
4 tbs. butter or margarine, melted and cooled
¼-⅓ cup chopped macadamias or walnuts, optional

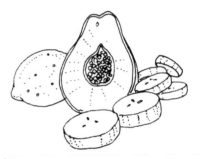

Beat egg white in a small bowl until stiff and set aside. Mix together dry ingredients and set aside. Combine egg yolk, juice, banana and butter. Add to dry ingredients, mixing until just blended. Add nuts, if desired, and fold in with beaten egg white until just mixed. Do not overbeat batter.

NUT AND NUT BUTTER WAFFLES

NUT WAFFLES

The walnut oil with walnuts is absolutely divine. Use your favorite nut - each has its own distinct taste and flavor. Suggested nuts: walnuts, almonds, pecans, brazil, macadamia, hazel, sunflower kernels, even mixed nuts!

1 egg, room temperature and separated
1¼ cups all purpose or whole wheat flour
1 tsp. baking powder
⅛ tsp. salt
1 tbs. brown sugar
¾ cup milk
4 tbs. butter or margarine, melted, or walnut oil
⅓ cup chopped nuts

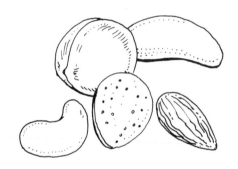

Beat egg white in a small bowl until stiff and set aside. Mix together dry ingredients and set aside. Combine egg yolk, milk and butter. Add to dry ingredients, mixing until just blended. Add nuts and fold in with beaten egg white until just mixed. Do not overbeat batter.

ORANGE NUT WAFFLES

This waffle will forever change your previous thoughts and expectations of waffles. This is a "must try."

1 egg, room temperature and separated
1 cup all purpose flour
1 tsp. baking powder
1/8 tsp. salt
1 tbs. sugar
1/8 tsp. orange peel
3/4 cup orange juice
4 tbs. butter or margarine, melted and cooled
1/4-1/3 cup ground nuts (walnuts or pecans)

Beat egg white in a small bowl until stiff and set aside. Mix together dry ingredients and set aside. Combine egg yolk, orange juice and melted butter. Add to dry ingredients, mixing until just blended. Add nuts and fold in with beaten egg white until just mixed. Do not overbeat batter.

HONEY NUT OATMEAL WAFFLES

3-4 waffles

The combination of honey, nuts and oatmeal has become a favorite in everything from cereal to bread. It shall now become a favorite of yours in waffles too! Bake longer for a crispier result.

1 egg, room temperature and separated
½ cup all purpose flour
¾ cup oats
1 tsp. baking powder
⅛ tsp. salt
¾ cup milk
2 tbs. honey
4 tbs. butter, melted and cooled
¼-⅓ cup chopped walnuts or pecans

Beat egg white in a small bowl until stiff and set aside. Mix together dry ingredients and set aside. Combine egg yolk, milk, honey and melted butter. Add to dry ingredients, mixing until just blended. Add nuts and fold in with beaten egg white until just mixed. Do not overbeat batter.

ALMOND BUTTER WAFFLES

This sweet, buttery waffle has lots of almond flavor.

1 egg, room temperature and separated
1 cup all purpose flour
1 tsp. baking powder
1/8 tsp. salt
2 tbs. sugar
2/3 cup milk
2 tsp. almond extract
6 tbs. butter or margarine, melted and cooled
1/4-1/3 cup chopped almonds

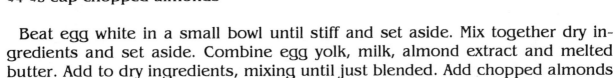

Beat egg white in a small bowl until stiff and set aside. Mix together dry ingredients and set aside. Combine egg yolk, milk, almond extract and melted butter. Add to dry ingredients, mixing until just blended. Add chopped almonds and fold in with beaten egg white until just mixed. Do not overbeat batter.

PEANUT BUTTER WAFFLES

*Kids (of all ages) flip over this. Serve with **Peanut Butter Honey**, page 149 or any of the other honey spreads, pages 148-150.*

1 egg, room temperature and separated
1 cup all purpose flour
1 tsp. baking powder
1/8 tsp. salt
3/4 cup milk
1/3 cup peanut butter
2 tbs. butter or margarine, melted and cooled
1 tbs. honey
1/4 cup chocolate chips, optional

Beat egg white in a small bowl until stiff and set aside. Mix together dry ingredients and set aside. Combine egg yolk, milk, peanut butter, honey and butter. Add to dry ingredients, mixing until just blended. Fold in chocolate chips, if desired, and beaten egg white until just mixed. Do not overbeat batter.

PEANUT BUTTER AND CHOCOLATE CHIP WAFFLES

Peanut butter and chocolate make a delicious combination, and this waffle is no exception!

1 egg, room temperature and
  separated
1 cup all purpose flour
1 tsp. baking powder
1/8 tsp. salt
1½ tsp. unsweetened cocoa
2/3 cup milk

¼ cup peanut butter
1 tbs. honey
2 tbs. butter or margarine, melted
  and cooled
3 tbs. peanut butter chips
3 tbs. chocolate chips

Beat egg white in a small bowl until stiff and set aside. Mix together dry ingredients and set aside. Combine egg yolk, milk, peanut butter, honey and butter. Add to dry ingredients, mixing until just blended. Add peanut butter and chocolate chips; fold in beaten egg white until just mixed. Do not overbeat batter.

Note: If desired, use a heaping 1/3 cup of one kind of chips and omit the other.

AMARANTH NUT WAFFLES

Amaranth has a nutty flavor to begin with - the nuts add to it.

1 egg, room temperature and separated
¾ cup all purpose flour
¼ cup amaranth flour
¼ cup oats (regular or quick cooking)
1 tsp. baking powder
⅛ tsp. salt
1 tbs. brown sugar
¾ cup milk
4 tbs. butter or margarine, melted and cooled
¼-⅓ cup chopped walnuts

Beat egg white in a small bowl until stiff and set aside. Mix together dry ingredients and set aside. Combine egg yolk, milk and butter. Add to dry ingredients, mixing until just blended. Add nuts and fold in with beaten egg white until just mixed. Do not overbeat batter.

ALMOND AMARETTO WAFFLES

A truly festive way to start a leisurely day.

1 egg, room temperature and separated
1¼ cups all purpose flour
1 tsp. baking powder
⅛ tsp. salt
1 tbs. brown sugar
⅓ cup amaretto
½ cup milk
4 tbs. butter or margarine melted and cooled
¼ cup chopped almonds

Beat egg white in a small bowl until stiff and set aside. Mix together dry ingredients and set aside. Combine egg yolk, amaretto, milk and butter. Add to dry ingredients, mixing until just blended. Add nuts and fold in with beaten egg white until just mixed. Do not overbeat batter.

CINNAMON CHOCOLATE NUT WAFFLES

3 waffles

The combination of cinnamon and chocolate is often found in Mexican cooking. Ole! If desired, nuts may, of course, be omitted.

1 egg, room temperature and separated
1¼ cups all purpose flour
1 tsp. baking powder
⅛ tsp. salt
3 tbs. sugar
¼ tsp. cinnamon
2 tbs. unsweetened cocoa
¾ cup milk
4 tbs. butter or margarine, melted and cooled
¼ cup chopped walnuts

Beat egg white in a small bowl until stiff and set aside. Mix together dry ingredients and set aside. Combine egg yolk, milk and butter. Add to dry ingredients, mixing until just blended. Add nuts and fold in with beaten egg white until just mixed. Do not overbeat batter.

PISTACHIO WAFFLES

These light, crispy waffles have a delicate flavoring of pistachios.

1 egg, room temperature and separated
1 cup all purpose flour
1 tsp. baking powder
⅛ tsp. salt
1 tbs. sugar
¾ cup milk
1 tsp. almond extract
4 tbs. butter or margarine, melted and cooled
¼-⅓ cup very finely chopped pistachios
2 tbs. raisins, optional

Beat egg white in a small bowl until stiff and set aside. Mix together dry ingredients and set aside. Combine egg yolk, milk, almond extract and butter. Add to dry ingredients, mixing until just blended. Add nuts, and raisins if desired; fold in with beaten egg white until just mixed. Do not overbeat batter.

DATE NUT WAFFLES

A sweet, cake like waffle. Some testers preferred it without any syrup.

1 egg, room temperature and separated
1¼ cups all purpose flour
1 tsp. baking powder
⅛ tsp. salt
1½ tsp. unsweetened cocoa
¾ cup milk
1 tbs. molasses
4 tbs. butter or margarine, melted and cooled
¼ cup chopped dates
¼ cup chopped walnuts

Beat egg white in a small bowl until stiff and set aside. Mix together dry ingredients and set aside. Combine egg yolk, milk, molasses and melted butter. Add to dry ingredients, mixing until just blended. Add dates and nuts; fold in with beaten egg white until just mixed. Do not overbeat batter.

CHOCOLATE RAISIN NUT WAFFLES

3 waffles

What a great combination. You may never return to "plain" waffles again!

1 egg, room temperature and separated
1 cup all purpose flour
1 tsp. baking powder
⅛ tsp. salt
1 tbs. brown sugar
1½ tsp. unsweetened cocoa
¾ cup milk
4 tbs. butter or margarine, melted and cooled
¼-⅓ cup raisins
¼ cup chopped walnuts or pecans

Beat egg white in a small bowl until stiff and set aside. Mix together dry ingredients and set aside. Combine egg yolk, milk and melted butter. Add to dry ingredients, mixing until just blended. Add raisins and nuts; fold in with beaten egg white until just mixed. Do not overbeat batter.

WALNUT RAISIN WAFFLES

The walnut oil imparts lots of great flavor to these waffles.

1 egg, room temperature and separated
1 cup all purpose flour or whole wheat flour
1 tsp. baking powder
⅛ tsp. salt
¾ cup milk
1 tbs. honey
3 tbs. walnut oil, or vegetable oil
¼ cup raisins
2-3 tbs. chopped walnuts

Beat egg white in a small bowl until stiff and set aside. Mix together dry ingredients and set aside. Combine egg yolk, milk, honey and oil. Add to dry ingredients, mixing until just blended. Add raisins and nuts; fold in with beaten egg white until just mixed. Do not overbeat batter.

CHOCOLATE NUT WAFFLES

3 waffles

This is an outrageously decadent chocolate waffle. Serve it with chocolate or maple syrup or as a dessert with ice cream.

1 egg, room temperature and separated
1¼ cups all purpose flour
1 tsp. baking powder
⅛ tsp. salt
¼ cup sweetened chocolate powder
¾ cup milk
4 tbs. butter or margarine melted and cooled
¼-⅓ cup chopped nuts
¼-⅓ cup chocolate chips, optional

Beat egg white in a small bowl until stiff and set aside. Mix together dry ingredients and set aside. Combine egg yolk, milk and butter. Add to dry ingredients, mixing until just blended. Add nuts and fold in with beaten egg white until just mixed. Do not overbeat batter.

Note: Sweetened chocolate powder is often sold as a hot chocolate powder mix.

BRAZIL NUT ORANGE WAFFLES

3 waffles

The combination of milk and orange juice is superb. Brazil nuts give these waffles pizzazz.

1 egg, room temperature and separated
1 cup all purpose flour
1 tsp. baking powder
⅛ tsp. salt
1 tbs. brown sugar
½ cup orange juice
¼ cup milk
4 tbs. butter or margarine, melted and cooled
¼-⅓ cup chopped brazil nuts

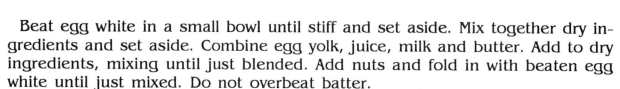

Beat egg white in a small bowl until stiff and set aside. Mix together dry ingredients and set aside. Combine egg yolk, juice, milk and butter. Add to dry ingredients, mixing until just blended. Add nuts and fold in with beaten egg white until just mixed. Do not overbeat batter.

PINEAPPLE NUT WAFFLES

3 waffles

This is an absolute "must try" for pineapple aficionados.

1 egg, room temperature and separated
1 cup all purpose flour
1 tsp. baking powder
⅛ tsp. salt
1 tbs. brown sugar
⅔ cup milk
¼ cup crushed pineapple, drained
4 tbs. butter or margarine, melted and cooled to warm (not hot)
¼ cup chopped nuts (walnuts, pecans, macadamias or almonds)

Beat egg white in a small bowl until stiff and set aside. Mix together dry ingredients and set aside. Combine egg yolk, milk, pineapple and butter. Add to dry ingredients, mixing until just blended. Add nuts and fold in with beaten egg white until just mixed. Do not overbeat batter.

ALMOND APRICOT WAFFLES

A must for apricot lovers, this is a unique, flavorful waffle.

1 egg, room temperature and
  separated
1 cup all purpose flour
1/3 cup oats
1 tsp. baking powder
1/8 tsp. salt
1/16 tsp. grated lemon peel
3/4 cup milk

1/2 tsp. almond extract
1 tbs. honey
4 tbs. butter or margarine, melted
  and cooled
2-3 tbs. diced dried apricots
2-3 tbs. chopped almonds
1-2 tbs. raisins, optional

Beat egg white in a small bowl until stiff and set aside. Mix together dry ingredients and set aside. Combine egg yolk, milk, almond extract, honey and butter. Add to dry ingredients, mixing until just blended. Add apricots, nuts, and raisins if desired; fold in with beaten egg white until just mixed. Do not overbeat batter.

CHOCOLATE ALMOND WAFFLES

Wow - this is out of this world. Not for a day you are trying to diet!

1 egg, room temperature and
  separated
1 cup all purpose flour
1 tsp. baking powder
1/8 tsp. salt
1/8 tsp. cinnamon
1/16 tsp. allspice

1/4 cup sweetened chocolate powder
2/3 cup milk
1 tbs. almond extract
4 tbs. butter or margarine melted
  and cooled
1/4-1/3 cup chopped almonds
1/4-1/3 cup chocolate chips, optional

Beat egg white in a small bowl until stiff and set aside. Mix together dry ingredients and set aside. Combine egg yolk, milk, almond extract and butter. Add to dry ingredients, mixing until just blended. Add nuts and chocolate chips; fold in with beaten egg white until just mixed. Do not overbeat batter.

Note: Sweetened chocolate powder is often sold as a hot chocolate powder mix.

YEAST WAFFLES

Waffles, just as many other baked foods, require a leavening agent. Most people assume that such an agent in waffle making must be the baking powder. Yeast has also been used, on occasion, in waffle making. You may be asking yourself why yeast should be used when it may seem like an awful lot of bother to proof it, etc. I found, during the testing for this book, that I actually preferred the yeast waffles and that they were easier to make on rushed mornings! The majority of the batter is made the evening before and all that needs to be done in the morning is to add the egg and in some cases, baking soda.

Please try at least one yeast waffle - don't let it scare you. Proofing the yeast sounds intimidating but it really is as easy as sprinkling the yeast granules over lukewarm water (105°-110°). You need not actually use a thermometer to determine if the water is the right temperature - just put a few drops on the inside of your wrist and see if it is "comfortably warm" - much as you would determine the warmth of a baby's bottle. You then sprinkle the yeast granules on top of the measured water (I do this in the bowl in which I will make the batter), cover it with a kitchen towel and set it aside for about 5 minutes while preparing the other ingredients.

BASIC YEAST WAFFLES

A wonderful variation on a basic waffle. Just a small amount of yeast makes these waffles rise nicely.

1/4 cup lukewarm water (105°-110°)
1/2 tsp. yeast (or about 1/5 package)
1 cup all purpose flour
1/8 tsp. salt
____

1 egg, room temperature and
  separated

1 tsp. sugar
1/2 cup milk, lukewarm
4 tbs. melted butter, cooled to room
  temperature

1/8 tsp. baking soda

Proof yeast in warm water for about 5 minutes. Meanwhile, mix together dry ingredients and set aside. Add milk and butter to yeast mixture. Add dry ingredients, mixing until just blended. Cover bowl with kitchen towel or plastic wrap and set in your cool oven or other draft-free location overnight.

In the morning, beat egg white in a small bowl until stiff and set aside. Mix egg yolk and baking soda into main mixture and then stir in egg white until just blended. Cook as usual.

YEASTED ORANGE NUT WAFFLES

A delightful twist to an old favorite.

¼ cup lukewarm water (105°-110°)
½ tsp. yeast (or about ⅕ package)
1 cup all purpose flour
⅛ tsp. salt
1 tsp. sugar

─────

1 egg, room temperature and
  separated

⅛ tsp. orange peel
½ cup orange juice, lukewarm
  (105°-110°)
4 tbs. melted butter, cooled to room
  temperature

¼ cup chopped nuts (walnuts,
  pecans, or almonds)

Proof yeast in warm water for about 5 minutes. Meanwhile, mix together dry ingredients and set aside. Add orange juice and butter to yeast mixture. Add dry ingredients, mixing until just blended. Cover bowl with kitchen towel or plastic wrap and set in your cool oven or other draft-free location overnight.

In the morning, beat egg white in a small bowl until stiff and set aside. Mix egg yolk and nuts into main mixture and then stir in egg white until just blended. Cook as usual.

YEASTED HONEY NUT OATMEAL WAFFLES   3 waffles

A delightful, sweet and nutty waffle.

¾ cup lukewarm water (105°-110°)
½ tsp. yeast (or about ⅕ package)
¾ cup all purpose flour
¾ cup oats (regular or quick cooking)

¼-½ tsp. salt
2 tbs. honey
4 tbs. melted butter cooled to room temperature

1 egg, room temperature and separated

¼ cup chopped nuts (walnuts, pecans, or almonds)

Proof yeast in warm water for about 5 minutes. Meanwhile, mix together dry ingredients and set aside. Add honey and butter to yeast mixture. Add dry ingredients, mixing until just blended. Cover bowl with kitchen towel or plastic wrap and set in your cool oven or other draft-free location overnight.

In the morning, beat egg white in a small bowl until stiff and set aside. Mix egg yolk and nuts into main mixture and then stir in egg white until just blended. Cook as usual.

YEASTED HONEY WAFFLES

Here is a sweeter variation of a basic waffle.

¼ cup lukewarm water (105°-110°)
½ tsp. yeast (or about ⅕ package)
1 cup all purpose flour
½ tsp. salt

⅓ cup milk, lukewarm
3 tbs. honey
4 tbs. melted butter, cooled to room
temperature

1 egg, room temperature and
separated

⅛ tsp. baking soda

Proof yeast in warm water for about 5 minutes. Meanwhile, mix together dry ingredients and set aside. Add milk, honey and butter to yeast mixture. Add dry ingredients, mixing until just blended. Cover bowl with kitchen towel or plastic wrap and set in your cool oven or other draft-free location overnight.

In the morning, beat egg white in a small bowl until stiff and set aside. Mix egg yolk and baking soda into main mixture and then stir in egg white until just blended. Cook as usual.

YEASTED CRANAPPLE WAFFLES

3 waffles

What a great, unique way to enjoy that favorite combination. Dried cranberries make this so easy to make and enjoy year-round.

¼ cup lukewarm water (105°-110°)
½ tsp. yeast (or about ⅕ package)
1 cup all purpose or whole wheat
 flour
¼ tsp. salt

1 egg, room temperature and
 separated

1 tbs. brown sugar
¼ tsp. cinnamon
½ cup apple juice, lukewarm
4 tbs. melted butter, cooled to room
 temperature

¼-⅓ cup dried cranberries, or finely
 chopped fresh, if available

Proof yeast in warm water for about 5 minutes. Meanwhile, mix together dry ingredients and set aside. Add juice and butter to yeast mixture. Add dry ingredients, mixing until just blended. Cover bowl with kitchen towel or plastic wrap and set in your cool oven or other draft-free location overnight.

In the morning, beat egg white in a small bowl until stiff and set aside. Mix egg yolk and cranberries into main mixture and then stir in egg white until just blended. Cook as usual.

YEASTED LEMON WAFFLES

*This recipe makes a very light, crispy and terrific waffle. Serve with lemon curd (may be warmed in the microwave) or **Lemon Creme**, page 152. This is sure to become a favorite. Do not cook too long.*

⅔ cup lukewarm water (105°-110°)
½ tsp. yeast (or about ⅕ package)
1 cup all purpose flour
¼ tsp. salt
1 tbs. sugar
_____

1 tsp. grated lemon peel
2 tbs. lemon juice
4 tbs. melted butter, cooled to room
    temperature

1 egg, room temperature and separated

Proof yeast in warm water for about 5 minutes. Meanwhile, mix together dry ingredients and set aside. Add juice and butter to yeast mixture. Add dry ingredients, mixing until just blended. Cover bowl with kitchen towel or plastic wrap and set in your cool oven or other draft-free location overnight.

In the morning, beat egg white in a small bowl until stiff and set aside. Mix egg yolk into main mixture and then stir in egg white until just blended. Cook as usual.

YEASTED WHIPPED CREAM WAFFLES

3 waffles

A light, fluffy and truly rich waffle. Not meant for calorie counting. Do not overcook.

¼ cup lukewarm water (105°-110°)
½ tsp. yeast (or about ⅕ package)
1 cup all purpose flour
¼ tsp. salt
¼ tsp. grated orange or lemon peel
_____

1 egg, room temperature and separated

½ cup whipping cream or heavy cream
2 tbs. confectioners' sugar
4 tbs. melted butter, cooled to room temperature

⅛ tsp. baking soda

Proof yeast in warm water for about 5 minutes. Meanwhile, whip cream and confectioners' sugar until thick. Mix together dry ingredients and set aside. Add whipped cream and butter to yeast mixture. Add dry ingredients, mixing until just blended. Cover bowl with kitchen towel or plastic wrap and set in your cool oven or other draft-free location overnight.

In the morning, beat egg white in a small bowl until stiff and set aside. Mix egg yolk and baking soda into main mixture and then stir in egg white until just blended. Cook as usual.

YEASTED HOMESTYLE WAFFLES

You'll enjoy this terrific, light and airy buttermilk waffle.

1/4 cup lukewarm water (105°-110°)
1/2 tsp. yeast (or about 1/5 package)
1 cup all purpose flour
1/8 tsp. salt
2 tsp. sugar

1/4 tsp. grated orange or lemon peel
2/3 cup buttermilk
2 tbs. melted butter cooled to room
 temperature

1 egg, room temperature and
 separated

1/8 tsp. baking soda

Proof yeast in warm water for about 5 minutes. Meanwhile, mix together dry ingredients and set aside. Add buttermilk and butter to yeast mixture. Add dry ingredients, mixing until just blended. Cover bowl with kitchen towel or plastic wrap and set in your cool oven or other draft-free location overnight.

In the morning, beat egg white in a small bowl until stiff and set aside. Mix egg yolk and baking soda into main mixture and then stir in egg white until just blended. Cook as usual.

CHRISTMAS MORNING WAFFLES

3 waffles

As the batter is made the evening before, this makes THE PERFECT breakfast for Christmas morning — a wonderful, festive waffle with minimal morning preparation. The taste is a cross between unbelievable and terrific. For real "eye appeal" use both red and green cherries which are available during the holiday season.

¼ cup lukewarm water (105°-110°)
½ tsp. yeast (or about ⅕ package)
1 cup all purpose flour
⅛ tsp. salt
1/16 tsp. nutmeg
1 tbs. confectioners' sugar
⅔ cup eggnog
2 tbs. melted butter cooled to room temperature

———

1 egg, room temperature and separated
⅛ tsp. baking soda
¼ cup maraschino cherries (about 10)
2 tbs. chopped nuts (any kind)

Proof yeast in warm water for about 5 minutes. Meanwhile, mix together dry ingredients and set aside. Add eggnog and butter to yeast mixture. Add dry ingredients, mixing until just blended. Cover bowl with kitchen towel or plastic wrap and set in your cool oven or other draft-free location overnight.

In the morning, beat egg white in a small bowl until stiff and set aside. Mix egg yolk, baking soda, cherries and nuts into main mixture and then stir in egg white until just blended. Cook as usual.

YEASTED WHOLE WHEAT AND BRAN WAFFLES

A great, nutritious waffle. Use for sandwiches or as a base for creamed chicken for a supper.

¾ cup lukewarm water (105°-110°)
½ tsp. yeast (or about ⅕ package)
1 cup whole wheat flour
¼ cup bran (oat, wheat or rice)

⅛ tsp. salt
4 tbs. melted butter, cooled to room temperature
1 tbs. honey

1 egg, room temperature and separated

Proof yeast in warm water for about 5 minutes. Meanwhile, mix together dry ingredients and set aside. Add honey and butter to yeast mixture. Add dry ingredients, mixing until just blended. Cover bowl with kitchen towel or plastic wrap and set in your cool oven or other draft-free location overnight.

In the morning, beat egg white in a small bowl until stiff and set aside. Mix egg yolk into main mixture and then stir in egg white until just blended. Cook as usual.

YEASTED BUCKWHEAT OATMEAL WAFFLES 3 waffles

A must for buckwheat lovers. The combination of buckwheat and oatmeal is an old favorite of many.

¼ cup lukewarm water (105°-110°)
½ tsp. yeast (or about ⅕ package)
½ cup buckwheat flour
1 cup oats (regular or quick cooking)
⅛ tsp. salt

½ cup milk, lukewarm (105°-110°)
4 tbs. melted butter cooled to room
  temperature
2 tbs. honey

1 egg, room temperature and
  separated

⅛ tsp. baking soda

Proof yeast in the water for about 5 minutes. Meanwhile, mix together dry ingredients and set aside. Add milk, honey and butter to yeast mixture. Add dry ingredients, mixing until just blended. Cover bowl with kitchen towel or plastic wrap and set in your cool oven or other draft-free location overnight.

In the morning, beat egg white in a small bowl until stiff and set aside. Mix egg yolk and baking soda into main mixture and then stir in egg white until just blended. Cook as usual.

TOPPINGS

Toppings for waffles may be varied from the basic maple syrup. A walk down the grocery aisle today will provide you with a wealth of ideas. These are some of the things you will find:

-an abundance of various fruit syrups
-applesauce
-apple butter
-confectioners' sugar — powder top
-fresh fruit — add confectioners' sugar, yogurt, or sauté in butter

-pourable fruit - an unsweetened fruit conserve found in health food stores or some larger grocery stores
-Creme Fraiche with fresh fruit
-lemon curd
-sauces — chocolate, butterscotch, etc.

Or serve your favorite waffle topped with ice cream or with freshly whipped cream and fruit.

In addition to sweets, use waffles in place of rice or noodles with your favorite dinner. It's a great way to enjoy the many whole grain waffles. In fact, anything you now serve over rice or noodles can be served over a delicious waffle for a wonderful variation. Some lunch or dinner suggestions include:

-Welsh rarebit
-pizza (pizza sauce, mozzarella, meats and/or vegetables)
-creamed chicken or meats

-chipped beef
-Stroganoff
-chili on a corn waffle
-creamed vegetables

CRANBERRY BUTTER

½ cup

Pure delight for a festive fall treat. This butter may also be served with bread during your Thanksgiving meal (shape with a related cookie cutter by filling the cookie cutter and chilling until firm. The cookie cutter may be removed by carefully pushing the butter out onto a plate or butter dish.)

1 stick unsalted butter, softened
2 tbs. confectioners' sugar
⅛ tsp. orange peel
3 tbs. chopped, fresh cranberries

Mix butter and confectioners' sugar in a food processor (steel blade) or blender until well blended. Add orange peel and cranberries and process or blend until just mixed. Shape with individual butter molds, cookie cutters or a ball. May be served chilled or room temperature. Butter may be refrigerated for several days.

SPICY BUTTER

Wonderful served with any apple waffle.

1 stick butter, softened   ½ tsp. pumpkin pie spice
1 tsp. honey

Combine ingredients until well blended. Serve at room temperature.

STRAWBERRY TOPPING

½ cup

This is absolutely delicious. One of the best.

4 oz. cream cheese, softened   1 tbs. pureed strawberries
½ cup confectioners' sugar

Cream softened cream cheese. Add sugar and blend well; fold in strawberries. Serve chilled or warmed from the microwave.

ORANGE TOPPING

½ cup

Serve with any basic or orange waffle. Delicious.

4 oz. cream cheese, softened
½ cup confectioners' sugar

4-5 mandarin orange segments
⅛ tsp. orange peel

Cream softened cream cheese and blend in remaining ingredients. Serve chilled or warmed from the microwave.

SAUTÉED APPLES

Servings: 2-4

*Absolutely superb - serve with **Spice Waffles**, page 60, or with any apple or basic waffle. May be served with or without maple syrup.*

1 medium apple, peeled and thinly
   sliced or diced

¼ tsp. cinnamon
1 tbs. butter or margarine

Melt butter or margarine in a small skillet over low heat. Add apple and cinnamon; sauté until crisp-tender.

Variation: MAPLE APPLES
   Omit cinnamon and use 2 tbs. of maple syrup.

BUTTERED PRESERVES

½ cup

A wonderful, easy topping. Serve softened, at room temperature.

4 tbs. unsalted butter, softened

¼ cup favorite fruit preserves
(strawberry, apricot, peach, etc.)

Cream butter and add preserves until well blended. I use the food processor with a steel blade, but a mixer or blender could also be used.

ORANGE SYRUP

¾ cup

This may be made in advance and kept in the refrigerator. Warm in a microwave or in a double boiler. Or, simmer over very low heat while you prepare your waffles.

½ cup orange juice
1 tsp. honey

1½ tsp. cornstarch
¼ cup mandarin orange segments

Heat orange juice, honey and cornstarch over medium heat, stirring constantly until thickened. Add orange segments and simmer for a few minutes or until ready to serve.

Variation: PINEAPPLE SYRUP

Substitute pineapple juice for the orange juice and drained crushed pineapple for the orange segments.

SPICED HONEY

A delectable syrup.

1/4 cup honey
1/2 tsp. cinnamon

1/8 tsp. nutmeg
1/8 tsp. cloves

Mix ingredients together and serve at room temperature. Keep refrigerated.

PAPAYA COCONUT

Here's another tropical delight.

1/4 cup papaya juice
1/4 cup coconut milk (canned)
2 tbs. water

1 1/2 tsp. cornstarch
1 tbs. coconut flakes

Heat papaya juice, coconut milk, water and cornstarch over low heat, stirring occassionally, until mixture thickens. Stir in coconut flakes until just mixed in and remove from heat. Serve warm. May be rewarmed in microwave.

FRUITED HONEY SYRUPS

¼ cup

Make creamy honey syrups using your favorite fruits. Use frozen fruit concentrates which have been thawed, or look for endless varieties of fruit concentrates at a well-stocked health food store.

¼ cup honey

1 tbs. fruit concentrate (orange, apple, grape, strawberry, blueberry, blackberry, raspberry

Mix honey and fruit concentrate together and serve at room temperature. Keep refrigerated.

PEANUT BUTTER AND HONEY

⅓ cup

Children will ask for waffles just to eat this topping! Try it with jelly in a sandwich.

¼ cup honey

2 tbs. peanut butter

Mix ingredients together and serve at room temperature. Keep refrigerated.

BANANA, PEANUT BUTTER AND HONEY

¼ cup

This is really a variation of the peanut butter and honey. But it will not keep, so smaller proportions are provided.

2 tbs. honey   1½-2 tsp. mashed banana
1 tbs. peanut butter

Mix ingredients together and serve immediately.

PEACH AND ORANGE SYRUP

1 cup

This astonishingly good syrup may be made in advance and warmed for serving.

1 can (8¼ oz.) peaches   2 tbs. sugar
¼ cup orange juice   ¼ tsp. cinnamon
1½ tsp. cornstarch   ⅛ tsp. grated orange peel

Drain peaches and process in a blender or food processor until smooth. Combine all ingredients in a small saucepan and heat over low heat, stirring often until sauce has thickened. Simmer until you are ready to serve or allow to cool and refrigerate until needed.

LEMON CREAM

¾ cup

*This topping is absolutely out of this world. A "must try" with **Yeasted Lemon Waffles,** page 135, or any basic waffle.*

4 oz. cream cheese, softened
¼ cup confectioners' sugar
1 tbs. lemon juice

½ tsp. grated lemon peel
1 tsp. poppy seeds, or to taste,
   optional

Cream softened cream cheese. Add remaining ingredients and mix until well-blended. Serve at room temperature or warmed in a microwave.

COCONUT DELIGHT

¾ cup

Serve with any tropical-island type waffle or any waffle which contains coconut. Of course, it is absolutely delicious with a plain, basic waffle also!

½ cup coconut milk (canned)
¼ cup water

2 tsp. cornstarch
1 tbs. coconut flakes

Heat coconut milk, water and cornstarch over low heat until mixture thickens. Stir in coconut flakes until just mixed and remove from heat. Serve warm. May be rewarmed in microwave.

INDEX

SERVE CREATIVE, EASY, NUTRITIOUS MEALS WITH NITTY GRITTY® COOKBOOKS

Waffles
The Coffee Book
The Bread Machine Cookbook
The Bread Machine Cookbook II
The Bread Machine Cookbook III
The Bread Machine Cookbook IV
The Sandwich Maker Cookbook
The Juicer Book
Bread Baking (traditional), revised
The Kid's Cookbook, revised
The Kid's Microwave Cookbook
15-Minute Meals for 1 or 2
Recipes for the 9x13 Pan
Turkey, the Magic Ingredient
Chocolate Cherry Tortes and Other Lowfat Delights

Lowfat American Favorites
Lowfat International Cuisine
The Hunk Cookbook
Now That's Italian!
Fabulous Fiber Cookery
Low Salt, Low Sugar, Low Fat Desserts
What's for Breakfast?
Healthy Cooking on the Run
Healthy Snacks for Kids
Creative Soups & Salads
Quick & Easy Pasta Recipes, revised
Muffins, Nut Breads and More
The Barbecue Book
The Wok
New Ways with Your Wok

Quiche & Soufflé Cookbook
Easy Microwave Cooking
Cooking for 1 or 2
Meals in Minutes
New Ways to Enjoy Chicken
Favorite Seafood Recipes
No Salt, No Sugar, No Fat Cookbook
New International Fondue Cookbook
Extra-Special Crockery Pot Recipes
Favorite Cookie Recipes
Authentic Mexican Cooking
Fisherman's Wharf Cookbook
The Creative Lunch Box

Write or call for our free catalog.
Bristol Publishing Enterprises, Inc.
P.O. Box 1737, San Leandro, CA 94577
(800)346-4889; in California (510)895-4461